DIVISION TO UNIFICATION IN IMPERIAL CHINA

The Three Kingdoms to the Tang Dynasty
(220 – 907)

Jing Liu

UNDERSTANDING
CHINA
THROUGH COMICS
VOLUME 2

A GRAPHIC NOVEL HISTORY FROM STONE BRIDGE PRESS

Berkeley CA

Published by
STONE BRIDGE PRESS
P.O. Box 8208 · Berkeley, California 94707
TEL 510-524-8732 · sbp@stonebridge.com · www.stonebridge.com

Text and illustrations © 2016 Jing Liu.

First edition, 2016.

Book design and layout by Linda Ronan.

Printed in the United States of America.

LIBRARY OF CONGRESS CATALOGING-IN-PUBLICATION DATA
Names: Liu, Jing (Author of graphic novels), author, illustrator.
Title: Foundations of Chinese civilization / Jing Liu.
Description: First edition. | Berkeley : Stone Bridge Press, 2016. | Series: Understanding China through comics | Includes bibliographical references and index.
Identifiers: LCCN 2016009755 (print) | LCCN 2016012382 (ebook) | ISBN 9781611720273 (alk. paper) | ISBN 9781611729184 (ebook)
Subjects: LCSH: China—History—Comic books, strips, etc. | Graphic novels.
Classification: LCC DS735 .L576 2016 (print) | LCC DS735 (ebook) | DDC 931—dc23
LC record available at http://lccn.loc.gov/2016009755

pISBN 978-1-61172-030-3
eISBN 978-1-61172-920-7

CONTENTS

TIMELINE

220 — Han dynasty falls
Age of Division begins

249 — Sima family launches coup and takes control of Wei court

265 — Jin dynasty is founded

280 — Jin dynasty invades the state of Wu and reunifies China

316 — Nomads overrun northern China

383 — Battle of Fei River

401 — Northern kingdom makes Buddhism the official state religion

420 — Jin dynasty falls
Northern and Southern Dynasties period begins

446 — Taoist emperor bans Buddhism

552 — Civil wars weaken the south

589 — Sui dynasty reunifies China, ending Northern and Southern
Dynasties period
Age of Division ends

612 — Emperor Yang leads 1 million troops to fight the Goguryeo

618 — Sui dynasty falls
Tang dynasty begins

690 — Wu Zetian founds Zhou dynasty

705 — Wu Zetian falls ill and is deposed by officials who proceed to
restore the Tang dynasty

755 — An Lushan rebellion

844 — Emperor Wuzong launches attack on Buddhism

907 — Tang dynasty falls

INTRODUCTION

When I first met Jing Liu in 1996, he immediately became a big part of my life. That was because when I started working at seminal expatriate publication *Beijing Scene*, upon my arrival he was not only my co-worker, but also my roommate. As such, you get to know someone quite quickly.

I remember clearly that Jing was asked to come up with sample illustrations for another author's book on Chinese philosophy, mostly from the perspective of idioms such as "Kill the Chicken to Frighten the Monkey." I don't remember the name of the book, but I recall vividly some of those drawings, and chuckle now even at the thought of them. It was clearly there that the seeds for this book and its earlier volume were sown.

Twenty years later, Jing's career has blossomed not only into a successful design business, but also now into the Understanding China through Comics series. Jing demonstrates his deep knowledge of China's vast history, but also shows that he perceives where foreigners may misunderstand events and their significance, and the nuances that will lead to a fuller knowledge of the subject. Both the young student and the old China hand can understand, and enjoy this illustrated and delightfully humorous look at one of the world's longest unbroken national histories and come away with a greater appreciation of the subject.

In Volume 2, it's fascinating to see how the concept of China evolved when the country was divided for the longest period of time in its history. Even after reunification by the Tang dynasty, Chinese culture continued to be influenced by people from what we consider to be "outside" of China. As Volume 1 discussed the essential origins of Chinese civilization, Volume 2 shows how dynamic outsiders pushed Chinese civilization to change in new and exciting ways.

From an author who is truly bicultural and bilingual comes a continuation of what may be the first look at Chinese history designed to amuse as much as educate. At the end of Volume 2, the good news is that there are still over 1,000 years to cover, so we still have much to which to look forward.

Steven Schwankert
Author, *Poseidon: China's Secret Salvage of Britain's Lost Submarine*

Previously in
Understanding China through Comics

Volume 1

Foundations of Chinese Civilization:
The Yellow Emperor to the Han Dynasty
(2697 BCE – 220 CE)

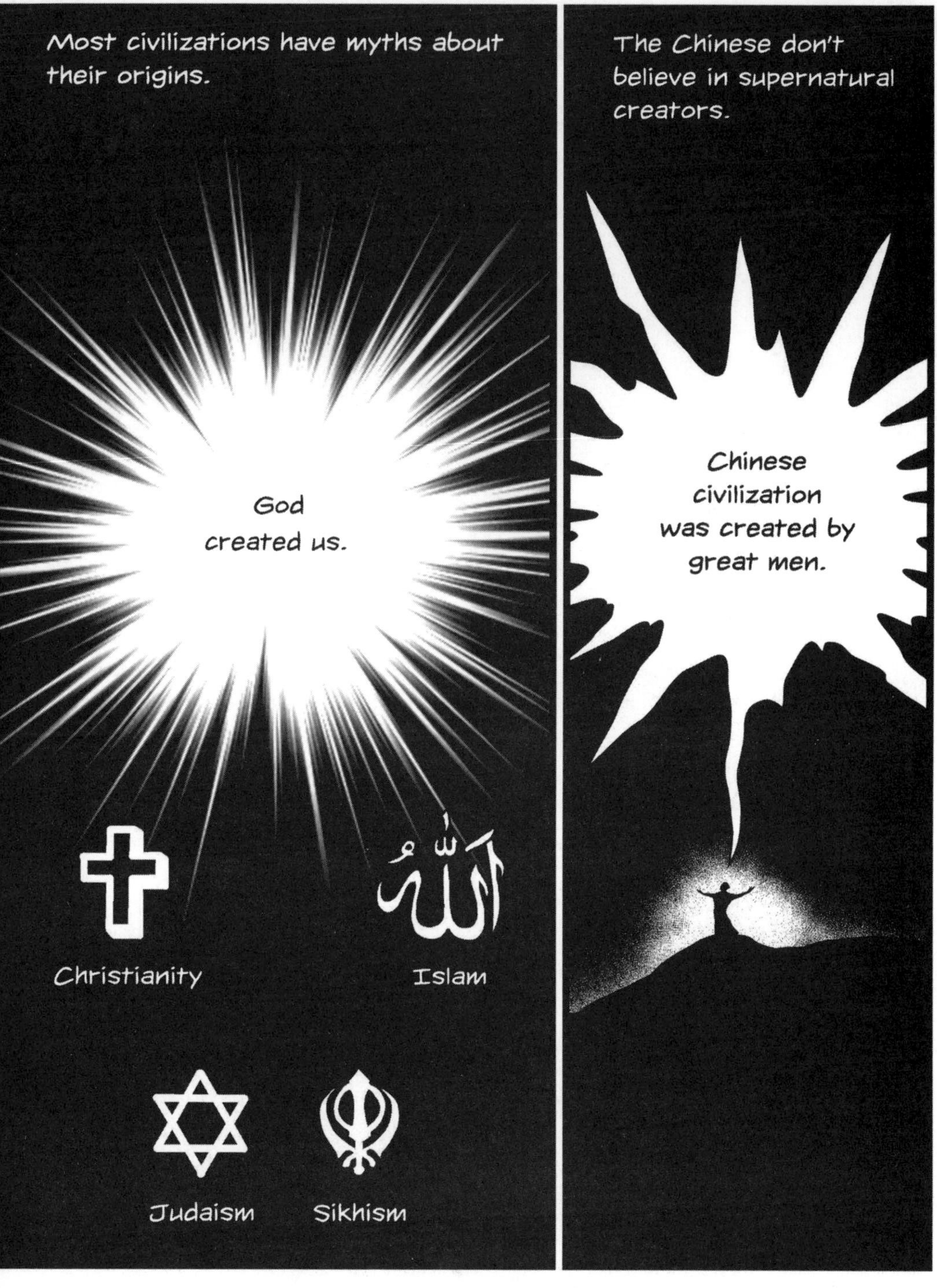
Most civilizations have myths about their origins.
God created us.
Christianity
Islam
Judaism
Sikhism
The Chinese don't believe in supernatural creators.
Chinese civilization was created by great men.

A good society must start with good people. To be good, people need to be inspired, not coerced. This is an important lesson for rulers.

Confucius

During the earliest years of Chinese civilization rulers like me had no interest in pondering Confucian questions such as how to rule benevolently. We had to fight!

In later years, Confucianism was an obvious choice for a state ideology. It taught subjects how to behave and trained good bureaucrats to work in the government.

But often officials supposed to be serving the emperor used their positions in the court to take power for themselves. They were corrupt and the people suffered as a result.

Down with the dynasty!

As dynasties rose and fell, a pattern was established
that would persist throughout Chinese history.
First dynasties prospered, then grew corrupt,
and finally collapsed. This is called the dynastic cycle.
Our story begins at the end of one of those cycles
just as the Han dynasty was falling apart.

UNDERSTANDING
CHINA
THROUGH COMICS

Volume

2

AGE OF DIVISION

220 – 589

The Yellow Turban rebellion broke out in 184 CE.

In the ensuing civil war, Chinese warlords hired foreign nomads as mercenaries.

However, these troops revolted and northern China fell under their control.

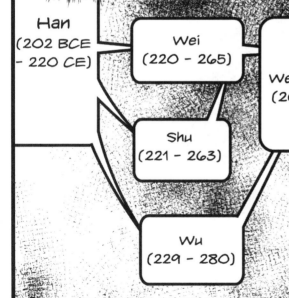

Han (202 BCE – 220 CE)

Wei (220 – 265)

Shu (221 – 263)

Wu (229 – 280)

Western Jin (265 – 316)

16 Nomadic Kingdoms (304 – 439)

Eastern Jin (317 – 420)

The Three Kingdoms (220 – 280)

When the 400-year Han rule came to an end,
China found itself divided once more, this time for another
400 years as warring factions struggled to reunify China.
Historians call this period the Age of Division.

The Age of Division ended
when the Sui took control of
the north and eventually
reunified China.

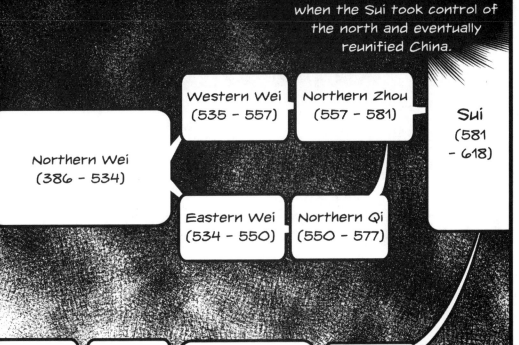

Western Wei
(535 – 557)

Northern Zhou
(557 – 581)

Sui
(581 – 618)

Northern Wei
(386 – 534)

Eastern Wei
(534 – 550)

Northern Qi
(550 – 577)

Liu Song
(420 – 479)

Qi
(479 – 502)

Liang
(502 – 557)

Chen
(557 – 589)

The Northern and Southern Dynasties
(420 – 589)

However, the fall of the Han didn't happen overnight. It took 36 years and was due to a number of different circumstances. In fact, understanding why the Han fell also helps explain why it was so hard for any one group to unify China during the Age of Division.

Last days of the Han

In 184, an epidemic in northern China, flooding of the Yellow River, famine, and heavy taxes all combined to trigger a massive rebellion.

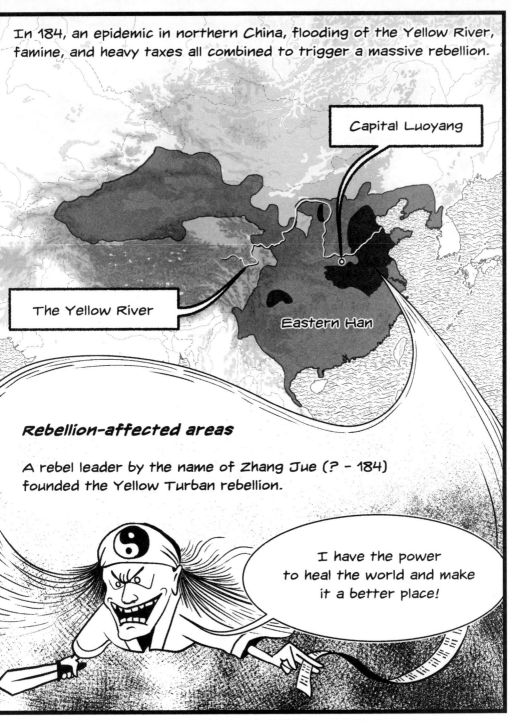

Capital Luoyang

The Yellow River

Eastern Han

Rebellion-affected areas

A rebel leader by the name of Zhang Jue (? – 184) founded the Yellow Turban rebellion.

I have the power to heal the world and make it a better place!

The Han court mobilized the entire country and crushed the main rebel force in only six months. However, smaller revolts continued for 21 years.

Eager to restore order, Emperor Ling of Han (156 – 189) empowered local governors.

Control your subjects, collect taxes, and make sure your army is big enough to fight the rebels.

After Emperor Ling died in 189, his wife's family fought with eunuchs over who would be the next emperor.

A general entered the capital and seized the imperial court for himself.

Dong Zhuo
(? – 192)

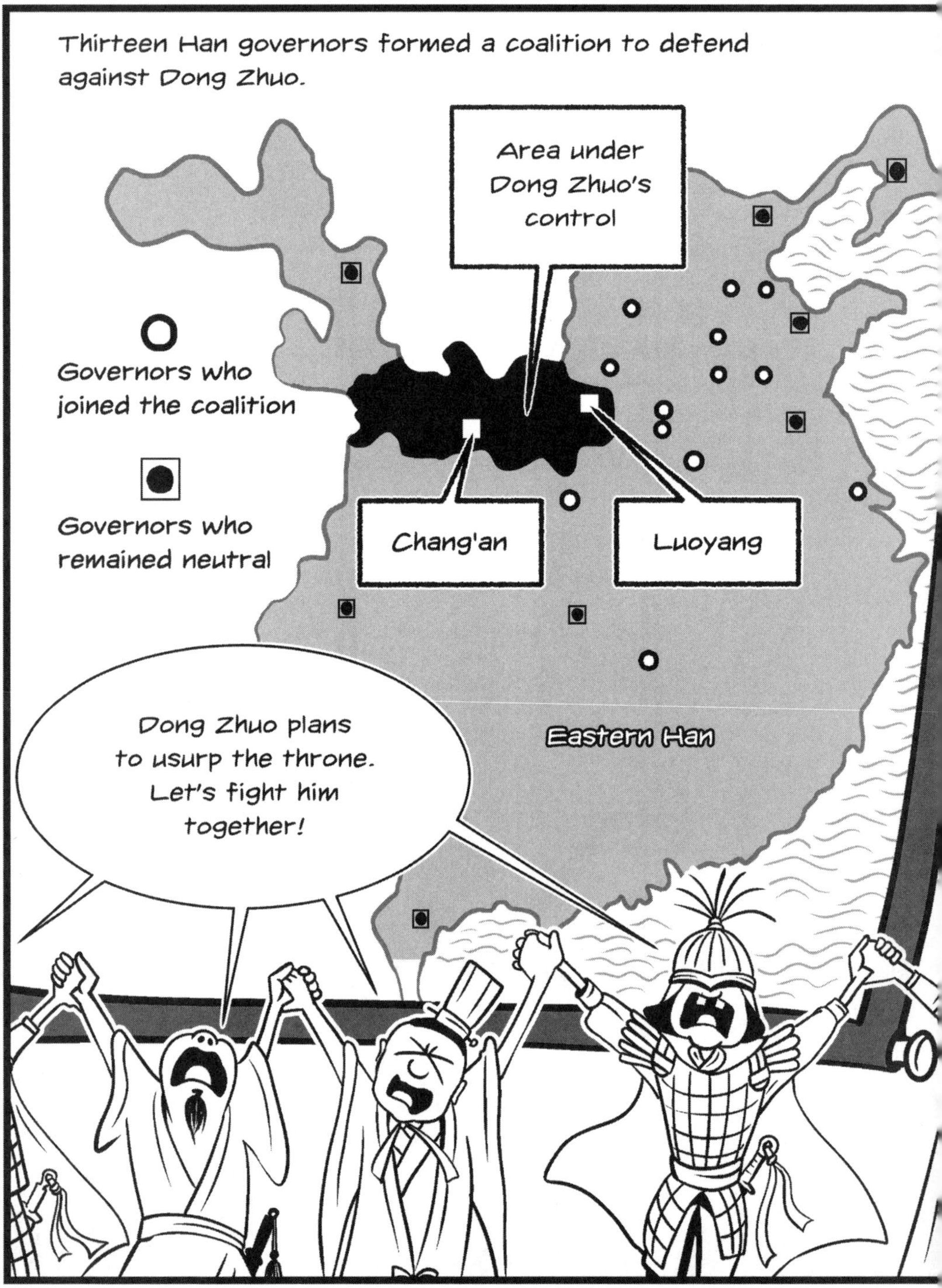
Thirteen Han governors formed a coalition to defend against Dong Zhuo.
Area under Dong Zhuo's control
Governors who joined the coalition
Governors who remained neutral
Chang'an
Luoyang
Eastern Han
Dong Zhuo plans to usurp the throne. Let's fight him together!

Dong Zhuo moved the capital from Luoyong to Chang'an.

Burn Luoyang to the ground! Leave nothing behind but smoke and ashes.

Two years later, Dong Zhuo was assassinated by his very own general.

Members of the anti-Dong coalition went on to seize land and establish their own states. These warlords fought more than 120 battles against each other over the next 30 years.

The Three Kingdoms

Of the many warlords fighting for supremacy in the early days after the fall of the Han, there were three big winners.

Cao Cao
(155 – 220)
A Han cavalry captain who fought against the Yellow Turban rebels and then laid the foundation for the Wei kingdom

Liu Bei
(161 – 223)
A minor noble who founded the Shu kingdom

Sun Quan
(182 – 252)
A young general who founded the Wu kingdom

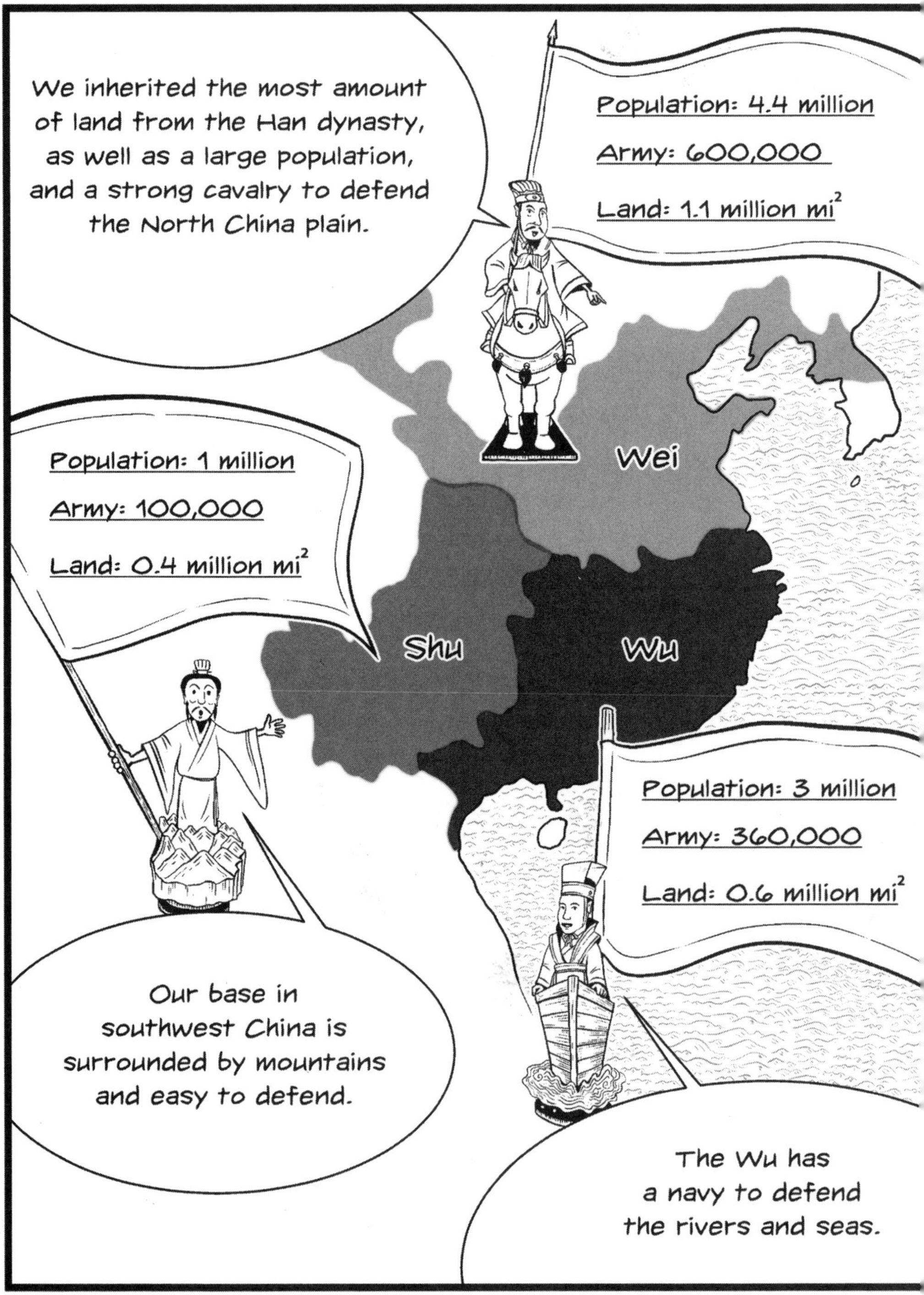

We inherited the most amount of land from the Han dynasty, as well as a large population, and a strong cavalry to defend the North China plain.
Population: 4.4 million
Army: 600,000
Land: 1.1 million mi^2
Wei
Population: 1 million
Army: 100,000
Land: 0.4 million mi^2
Shu
Wu
Population: 3 million
Army: 360,000
Land: 0.6 million mi^2
Our base in southwest China is surrounded by mountains and easy to defend.
The Wu has a navy to defend the rivers and seas.

The resources of these three states determined their strategies as they tried to unify China.

Shu strategy: Offense as defense

As the weakest state, the only way for us to survive is to use maximum effort to defeat the strongest kingdom, Wei, as quickly as possible.

Sort of how the smallest dogs always bark the loudest...

To invade the north, we must ally with the Wu Kingdom.

In a span of 40 years, the Shu launched 16 military expeditions against the Wei.

Wei strategy: Slow attrition

The Wei took a defensive position to prolong the war with the Shu.

Our advantage in resources will allow us to gradually wear out our enemies.

At the same time, we will keep the Wu busy by occasionally attacking them.

Wu strategy: Self-preservation

For the most part, the Wu acted together with the Shu to resist the stronger Wei.

I married my sister to the Shu ruler to strengthen our alliance.

However, when the Shu had a chance to defeat the Wei in 219, the Wu attacked its ally from behind.

We can't let the Shu grow too big!

The Shu retaliated in full...

...only to be defeated by the Wu and lose 80% of its army.

Within a year, both sides had come to their senses and the Shu–Wu alliance was restored.

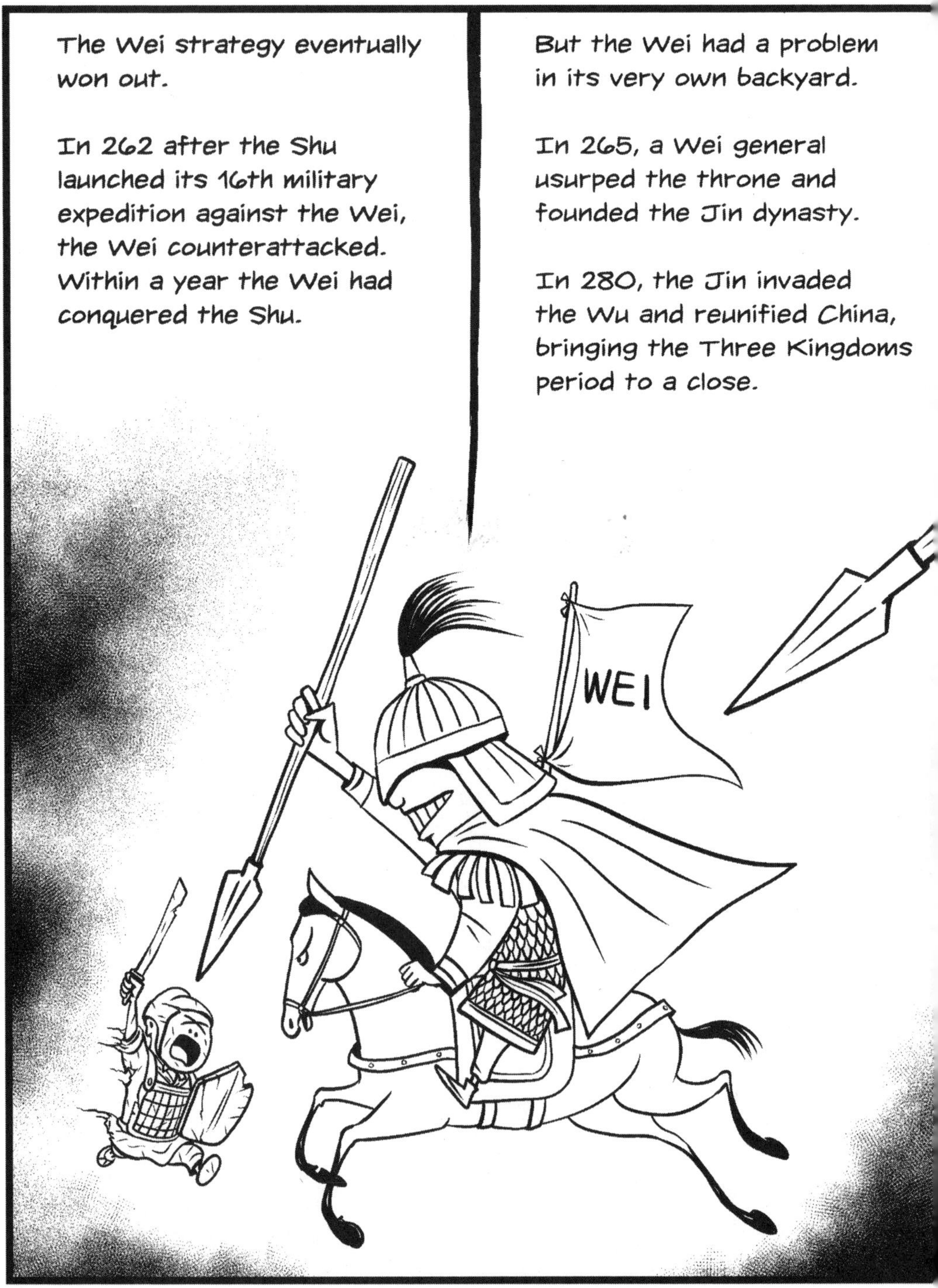
The Wei strategy eventually won out.
In 262 after the Shu launched its 16th military expedition against the Wei, the Wei counterattacked. Within a year the Wei had conquered the Shu.
But the Wei had a problem in its very own backyard.
In 265, a Wei general usurped the throne and founded the Jin dynasty.
In 280, the Jin invaded the Wu and reunified China, bringing the Three Kingdoms period to a close.
WEI

Today in China, the Three Kingdoms is one of the best-known periods in Chinese history thanks to a novel published in the 14th century.

This book, *The Romance of the Three Kingdoms*, tells of heroes and villains, battle tactics and political strategy, and loyalty and betrayal on a massive scale.

It contained 1,191 characters, a record among all Chinese classical novels.

The Romance of the Three Kingdoms

三国演义

The book is famous for its opening line: Anything long divided will surely unite, and anything long united will surely divide.

话说天下大势，分久必合，合久必分。

Doesn't that sound similar to the idea of the dynastic cycle?

Rise of the aristocracy

In reality, the Three Kingdoms period was a horrifically violent time. Constant war wiped out over 60% of the population.

50 million in
late Han (184)

16 million
in early Jin (280)

Poor families looked
to local warlords
for protection.

Adult males
must serve as soldiers,
everyone else must provide
food and supplies
for our army.

To make sure
we have enough manpower
boys must marry before the age of 16.
Girls can only marry men
in the military.

Rich families built fortresses and hired private armies to defend themselves.

As many as 10,000 people could live inside these fortresses with walls as tall as those of the imperial capital.

Communities had to learn to be self-sufficient, since it was dangerous to rely on trade with others that could be disrupted by war.

Fortresses were surrounded by farms, ponds, breweries, and mills that provided a number of goods, including crops, meat, wine, clothing, bricks, firewood, and candles.

We work for our lord.
In return, we receive a salary
or small piece of land.

The lords of these fortresses were nobles, high officials, senior scholars, and other wealthy families of Han dynasty lineage.

Their large homes were states within a state, and marked the rise of a powerful aristocratic class during a time in which the central government was very weak.

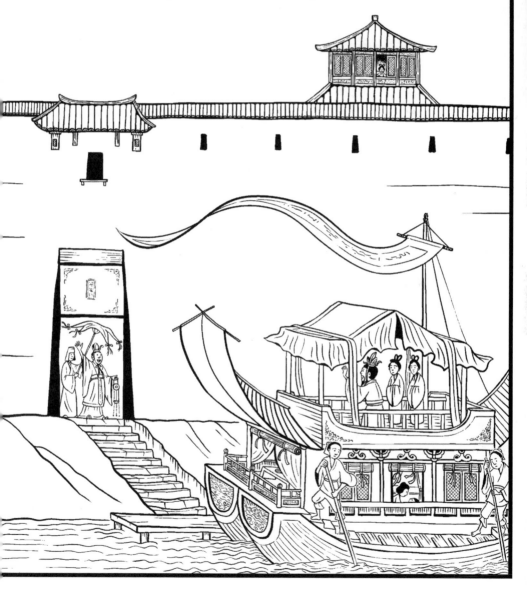

During the Three Kingdoms period, the Shu, Wei, and Wu competed to gain the support of these wealthy families.

The Wei state went as far as creating a political system to attract great families.

If you support our war efforts by providing us food and laborers, you will be exempt from taxes and your children will be given important government jobs.

Welcome to the Nine-rank System.

You may nominate candidates for positions in the government as officials.

A judge will rank each applicant's suitability based on their ancestry, ability, morality, and reputation in the community. Each applicant will then be given a rank between 1 and 9.

Through the Nine-rank System the Sima family were able to put their relatives in positions to control the appointment of government officials. In this way, they began to take over the Wei state by filling the court with family members and friends.

Profound Learning movement

While the Sima family plotted to take control of the Wei kingdom, many Wei aristocrats were being drawn to a new philosophy called Profound Learning.

During the Eastern Han, Confucianism had become a tool used by the eunuchs and their followers.

The problem is not Confucianism itself.

The problem is that the Han government put too much focus on managing society from the top down.

Confucius believed that a good society must start with good people.

We should help each individual person become good. That way we can improve our nation from the bottom up.

A government's role is to stay strong and lead the country, but not interfere in the lives of individuals.

We can set forth a series of policies to rule the people based on this principle.

Cao Shuang
(? – 249),
Wei regent

Allow freedom of expression by establishing a new curriculum for schools and a new way of teaching.

He Yan
(? – 249),
Minister of Personnel

Improve public works and social welfare.

Make sure to not tax the people too heavily and avoid wasteful construction projects and unnecessary wars.

Xiahou Xuan
(209 – 254),
Wei minister

Wang Bi
(226 – 249),
scholar

In order to reduce expenses we'll get rid of unnecessary bureaucracy by cutting down on the number of governors.

In 249, before the Profound Learning movement had a chance to impact the Wei government, the Sima family launched a coup and took control of the Wei court.

To silence opposition, the Sima executed over 3,000 scholars, officials, and family members, including many Profound Learners.

Some officials and scholars quit their government positions in protest against the actions of the Sima family.

A group of Profound Learners often gathered in a bamboo grove near the Wei capital.

A gentleman should withdraw from politics and learn to find happiness in poetry, music, art, and philosophy.

These Profound Learners took their philosophical movement to new extremes.

Words and images can only convey basic meaning.

How can we go further and unveil the fundamental truth of everything?

Several resorted to using a type of drug called the Powder of Five Minerals, which induced hallucinations, fevers, and visions.

I'm hot with the freedom of pure thought!

Chinese drinking tradition, influenced by Profound Learning, started to take shape. Heavy drinking was praised as an achievement.

Philosophical debates lift one's spirit, while spirits cultivate one's taste.

A man should stand as straight as a pine tree.

When drunk, he should fall like the avalanche on a great mountain.

A man of principle should go all the way in drink and song and live a carefree life in pursuit of the ultimate truth.

The Sima clan was quick to react.

These Profound Learners are out of control!

Summon their leader to the court.

No! I refuse to obey you.

Ji Kang (223 – 262), philosopher and musician

Kill him as a warning to the others.

Let me first finish this song and then slay me. OK?

People secretly honored Ji Kang and his fellow Profound Learners as the Seven Sages of the Bamboo Grove.

Once the Sima clan had secured control of the Wei court, they led the Wei army against the Shu. The Wei defeated the Shu in 263. The victory won the Sima family enormous credit.

Two years later in 265, Sima Yan (236 – 290) removed the Wei ruler and established the Jin dynasty.

In 280, the Jin defeated the Wu and reunified China.

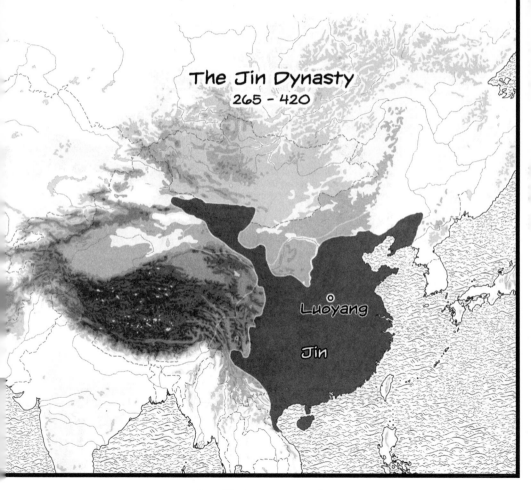

The Jin Dynasty
265 – 420

Luoyang

Jin

Sima Yan was feeling generous and gave himself the title Emperor Wu.

Since the war is over and soldiers will be returning home, let's give each family 100 mu* of land.

In return, each family must pay half their harvest as tax.

* 1 mu = 0.165 acres

Half of our harvest?

Well, in the late Three Kingdoms farmers were taxed at 70% and the land was owned by the state. This is a great deal!

Nobles and officials received at least 10 times more land than the commoners and paid fewer taxes.

Their luxurious lifestyles were documented by a publication called *A New Account of the Tales of the World.*

Once a member of the imperial family used 12 miles of silk screens as part of a ceremony to greet his friend.

The next time these men met, the official used 15 miles of silk.

You're so much richer than me.

Well, I'm just a mid-level official. I'm a pauper compared to some of these other guys.

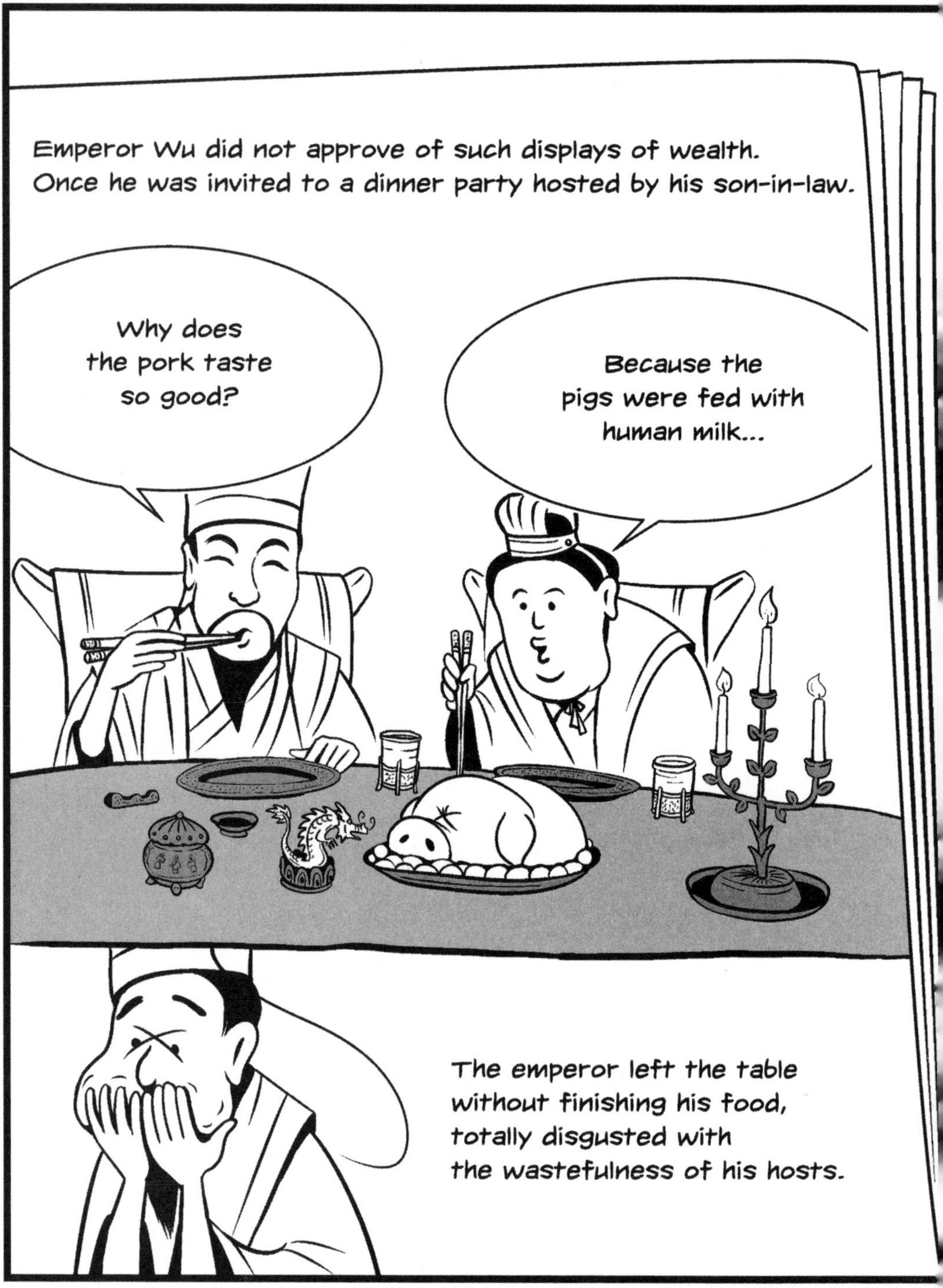
Emperor Wu did not approve of such displays of wealth. Once he was invited to a dinner party hosted by his son-in-law.
Why does the pork taste so good?
Because the pigs were fed with human milk...
The emperor left the table without finishing his food, totally disgusted with the wastefulness of his hosts.

There were two major threats to Emperor Wu's power.
Both were vestiges of the Three Kingdoms period.

Local aristocrats who owned massive estates and controlled private armies that deprived the state of tax income and manpower

Semi-independent nomad mercenaries in the Chinese military

Xiongnu

Xianbei

Jie

Qiang

Di

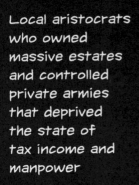

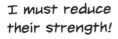
I must reduce their strength!

Barbarians conquer the capital

In 290, Emperor Wu died before
fully consolidating the young Jin dynasty.

The wife and regent of the next emperor
soon began struggling for control of the court.

Eight Jin princes also jumped into the conflict.

Local aristocrats chose sides and
the imperial power struggle soon escalated to a 15-year civil war.

Nomad mercenaries compounded the problem
by embarking on a 12-year rebellion.

In only a decade after being reunified by the Jin,
China once again sank into chaos.

When the nomad mercenaries took the Jin capital (Luoyang) in 311 and the capital-in-exile (Chang'an) in 316, they captured two Jin emperors. The Jin court retreated to the south, ending what historians consider to be the Western Jin dynasty.

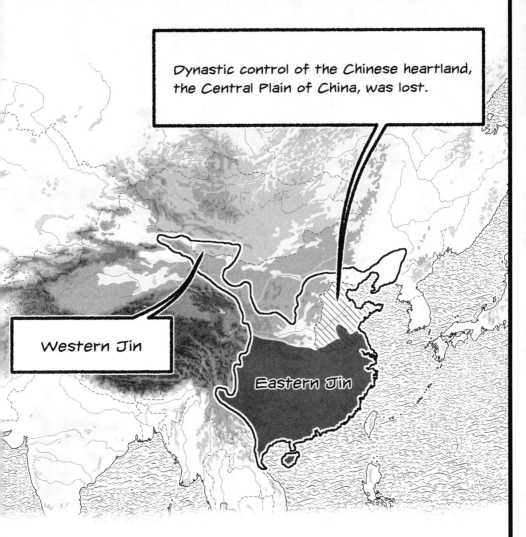

Dynastic control of the Chinese heartland, the Central Plain of China, was lost.

Western Jin

Eastern Jin

In 317, a Jin prince in south China claimed to be the true heir to the throne. This marked the beginning of the Eastern Jin dynasty.

Chinese culture moves south

Around 1/8 of the 7 million people living in northern China packed up their bags and fled south.

The south already has 5.4 million people.

Where can these immigrants live?

We can turn less populated areas into zones for immigrants.

Refugees can stay there, farm to feed themselves, and pay taxes.

Northern aristocrats were put in charge of the immigrant zones.

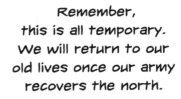

I miss home. Let's name this new place after our hometown in northern China.

Remember, this is all temporary. We will return to our old lives once our army recovers the north.

Most never saw their homes again.

With the cradle of Chinese civilization lost to those northern "barbarians," southern aristocrats saw themselves as defenders of the true Chinese way of life.

Chinese culture developed in new and important ways during the Eastern Jin dynasty.

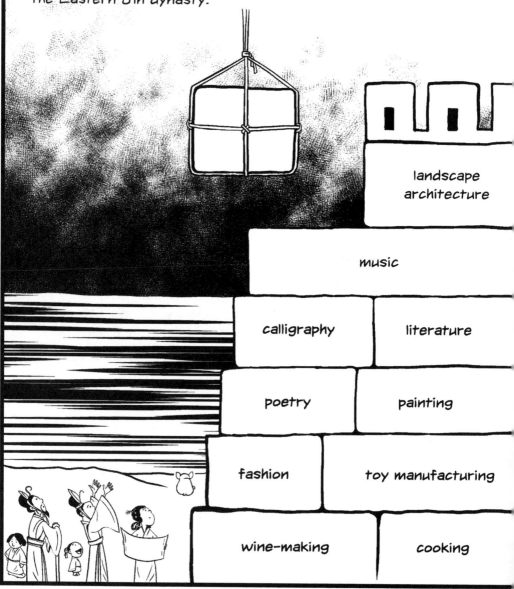

landscape architecture

music

calligraphy

literature

poetry

painting

fashion

toy manufacturing

wine-making

cooking

One of the most renowned literary works of the Eastern Jin was called *Preface to the Poems Composed at the Orchard Pavilion*. This work was written by Wang Xizhi, a military general from a noble family.

Wang Xizhi (303 – 361), the "Sage" of Chinese calligraphy

In the book he wrote:

Times can change
and the world can change,
but people's fundamental nature will remain the same.

Life is short
and one's definition of happiness often changes,
but everyone will have to face this question one day.

What is the meaning of life?

Battle of Fei River

The Eastern Jin fought 13 campaigns over the next 100 years to retake the north. The nomad kingdoms, however, held fast, posing a serious threat to the southern Chinese dynasty.

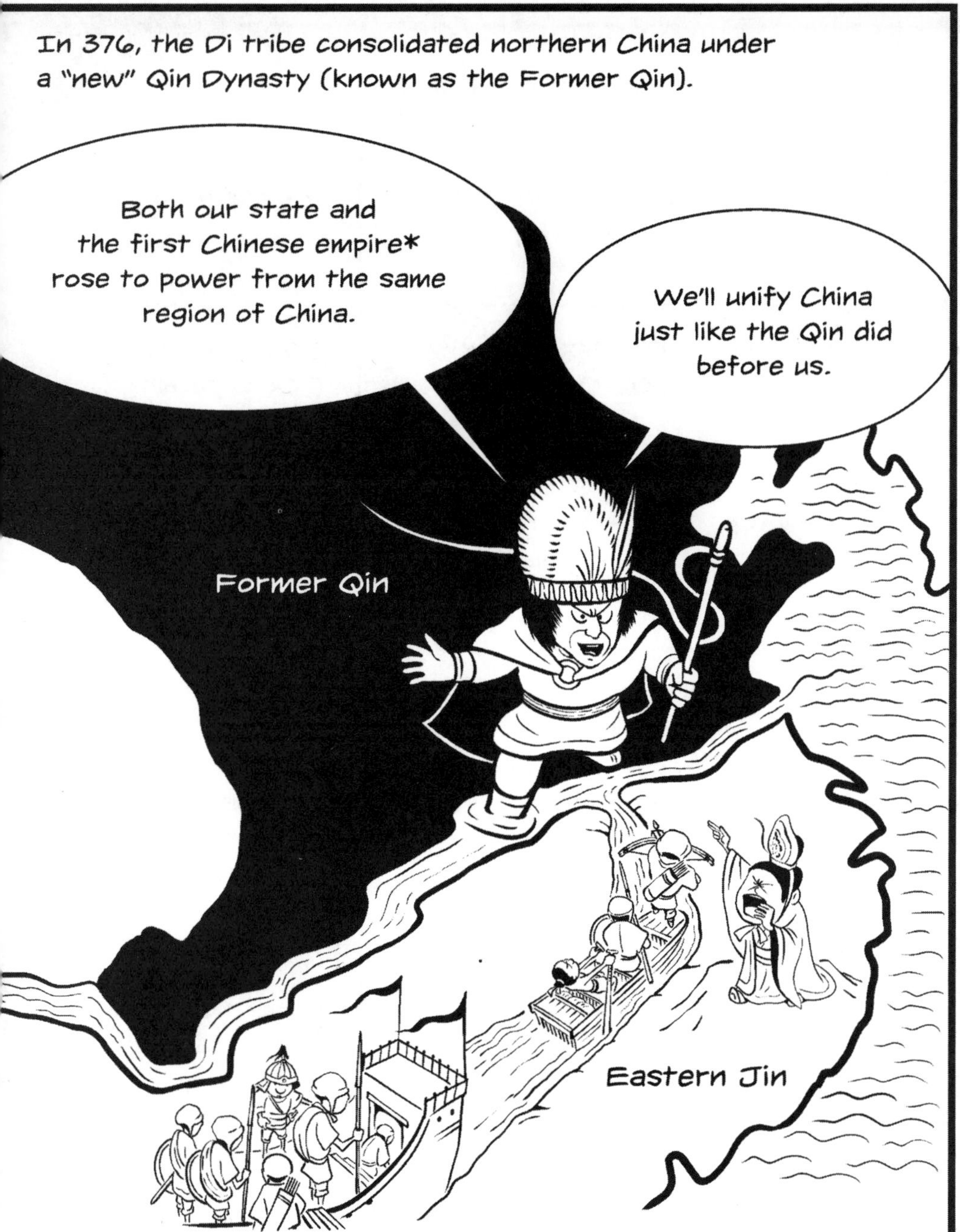
In 376, the Di tribe consolidated northern China under a "new" Qin Dynasty (known as the Former Qin).
Both our state and the first Chinese empire* rose to power from the same region of China.
We'll unify China just like the Qin did before us.
Former Qin
Eastern Jin
* the Qin dynasty of the 3rd century BCE

In 383, the two sides met at Fei River.

	Former Qin (North)	**Eastern Jin** (South)
Strength	600,000 infantry 270,000 cavalry	80,000 infantry 5,000 cavalry
Commanders	The Former Qin emperor and his younger brother	Aristocrats from 3 major clans
Soldiers	Di tribesmen plus troops of 5 ethnicities	Private armies of different clans, Chinese bandits, and northern refugees
Strategy	Use the Eastern Jin as an external enemy to help unite different tribes.	Force the enemy into a stalemate and then look for opportunities to divide and conquer.

Before the battle, the Qin emperor sent a captured Jin official to persuade the Chinese to surrender.

Tell them our army is so huge that we could dam the longest Chinese river by simply throwing our whips into it.

The official arrived in the Eastern Jin.

The Former Qin army is huge, but most men have little loyalty to their emperor, and internal coordination is very poor.

They're mounting an attack now with 15,000 troops, but they're advancing too fast, exposing their flank...

In October of 383, the Jin army ambushed the advance troops of the Former Qin. Afterwards, the Jin army formed a thin line east of the Fei River, intentionally visible to the enemy.

The Former Qin emperor was befuddled.

A message from the Eastern Jin commander...

Please move your troops *slightly* backward, so we can cross the river and fight you. *We'll die for our country!*

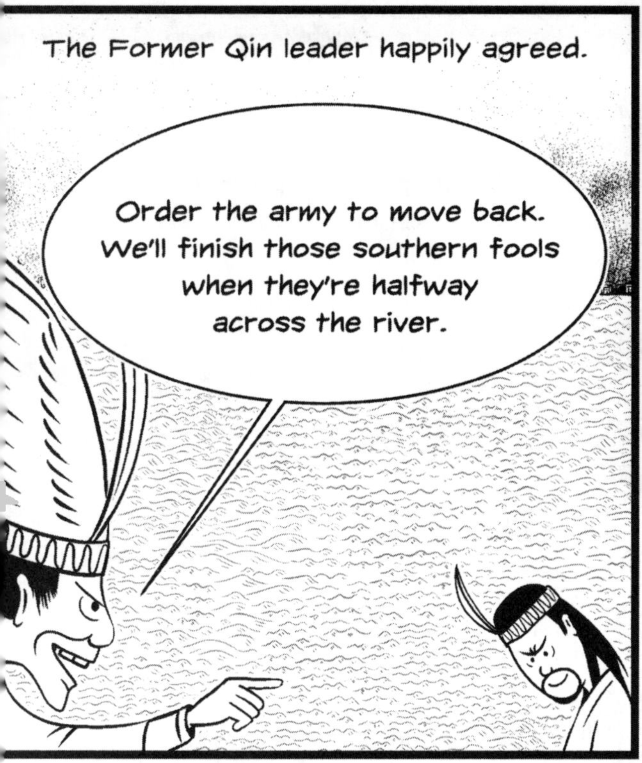
The Former Qin leader happily agreed.
Order the army to move back. We'll finish those southern fools when they're halfway across the river.

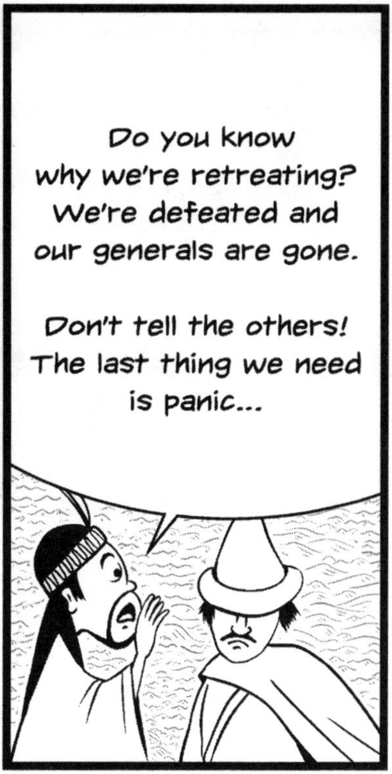
Do you know why we're retreating? We're defeated and our generals are gone.
Don't tell the others! The last thing we need is panic...

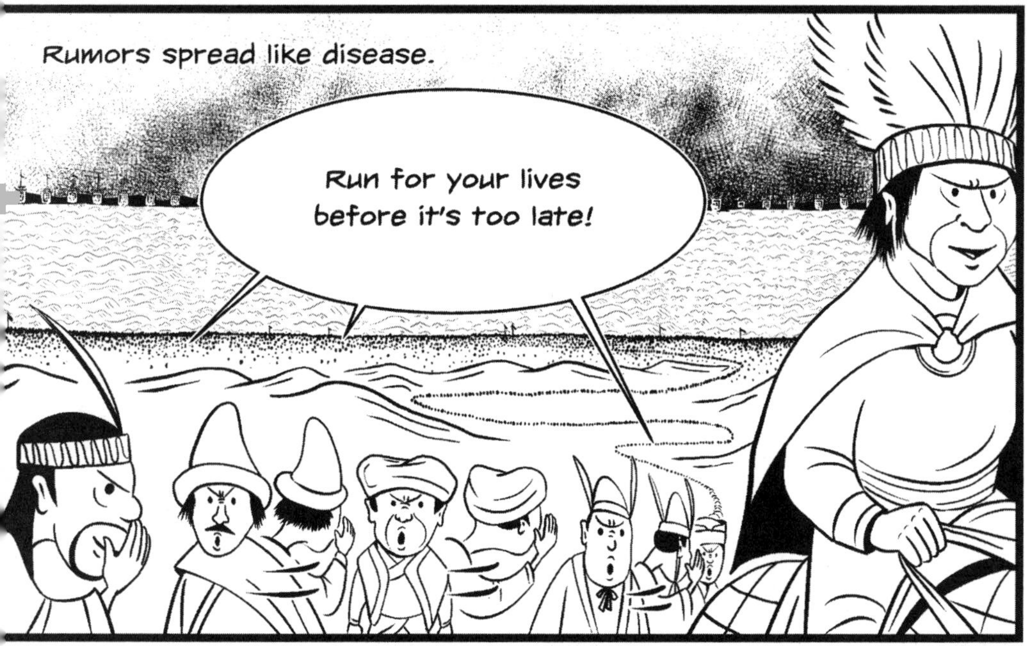
Rumors spread like disease.
Run for your lives before it's too late!

When the Jin started to cross the river,
the Former Qin army panicked.
Most deserted the battlefield without putting up a fight.
Of the 870,000 soldiers, only 100,000 ever came back.

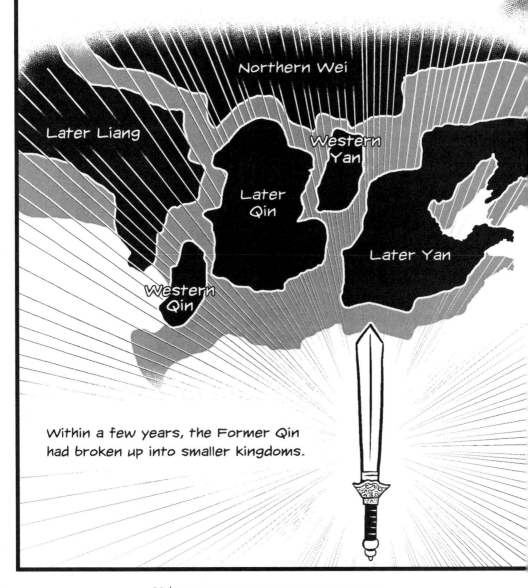

Within a few years, the Former Qin
had broken up into smaller kingdoms.

The Northern and Southern dynasties
420 – 589

After the Battle of Fei River, the Eastern Jin army continued
to play an important role in the fight against the north.
As the army grew in popularity and importance with each
military victory, so did its commanders.

In 420, one commander decided to overthrow the Jin dynasty
and establish the Song dynasty in southern China.
The Song was also known as the Liu Song.

In 439, the Xianbei tribe unified northern China under
the Wei dynasty, also known as the Northern Wei.

Both dynasties claimed to be the legitimate ruler of China,
beginning a period in Chinese history known as
the Northern and Southern dynasties.

Northern Wei

Liu Song

In northern China, millions of commoners were under constant threat.

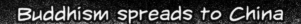

war

heavy taxation

military conscription

hard labor

In this time of widespread suffering, a religion from a foreign land called Buddhism offered a remedy to suffering that was radically different from traditional Chinese solutions.

Why is there so much suffering?

Confucianism:
We will build a good government to end the suffering.

Taoism:
Suffering is an inescapable aspect of human life, learn to live with it.

Buddhism:
Yes, suffering is part of life. But you can end it!

Practice spiritual exercises to detach yourself from desire. Desire is the source of suffering.

Buddhism also addressed issues of life and death in a way no Chinese belief system had before.

What happens after we die?

Confucianism:

We don't fully understand life yet so how can we know about death?

Taoism:

Taoists seek to attain immortality by alchemy and meditation.

But only rich people have the time and resources to experiment with alchemy.

Buddhism:

People are trapped in a cycle of birth, death, and rebirth.

To be reborn to a better life, you must do good things in your current life.

If you work hard enough, you will eventually achieve enlightenment and become a Buddha.

The founder of Buddhism, Shakyamuni Buddha, or the Enlightened One, lived at the same time as Confucius.

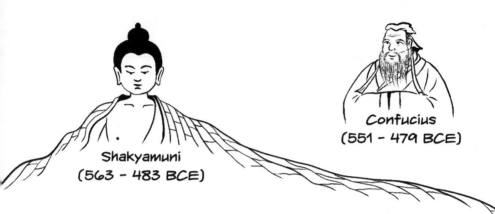

Confucius
(551 – 479 BCE)

Shakyamuni
(563 – 483 BCE)

His teachings were first brought to China from India during the Han dynasty by monks traveling along the Silk Road. In early translations of Buddhist sutras, Indian monks used many Taoist terms to introduce Buddhist ideas to Chinese people.

Taoism shares a similar concept with Buddhism.

That concept is emptiness.

Buddhists meditate on emptiness, which in turn leads to enlightenment.

Taoists use meditation to empty the mind of all desire not fit for the Tao.

Emptiness is not nothingness. It is the wisdom to understand the ultimate truth, which lies beneath the day-to-day reality we experience.

During the Age of Division, Buddhism gained a strong following in many different states.

In 319, a ruler of the Later Zhao, one of the 16 Nomadic Kingdoms, made Master Fotudeng (232 – 348) his chief advisor.

The next ruler even made it legal for Chinese people to become monks.

Many jumped at the opportunity to work in Buddhist temples, in part to avoid heavy taxes and military service.

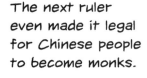

Your country has many ethnic groups, including your Jie people and the Han Chinese.

You need an ideology acceptable to everyone.

In 401, a ruler of
the Later Qin,
another one of the
16 Nomadic Kingdoms,
made Buddhism
the state religion
and gave monk
Kumarajiva (334 – 413)
the title of
State Teacher.

Buddhist study and
meditation were not easy.
A Chinese scholar-turned-monk,
Tanluan (476 – 542), decided to
find a short cut to enlightenment.

With the support of
a Northern Wei ruler and
help from Indian monks,
Tanluan founded
Pure Land Buddhism.

Kumarajiva translated
many Buddhist texts.
This made Buddhism
so accessible that
soon 90% of the
Later Qin population
was aware of its practices.

Any true follower
will be reborn into
the Pure Land of Utmost Bliss.

There, you can continue
working to become enlightened
without any deadlines
or pressure.

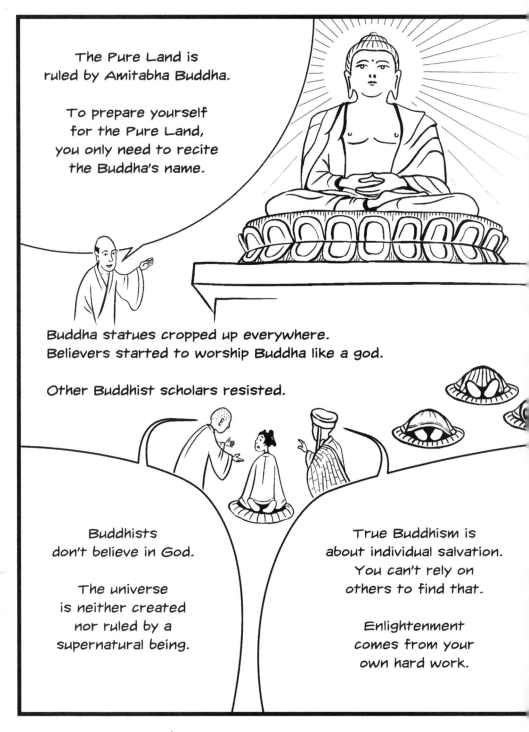

The Pure Land is ruled by Amitabha Buddha.

To prepare yourself for the Pure Land, you only need to recite the Buddha's name.

Buddha statues cropped up everywhere.
Believers started to worship Buddha like a god.

Other Buddhist scholars resisted.

Buddhists don't believe in God.

The universe is neither created nor ruled by a supernatural being.

True Buddhism is about individual salvation. You can't rely on others to find that.

Enlightenment comes from your own hard work.

Nonetheless, Pure Land Buddhism became very popular among Chinese. There were two million monks and nuns practicing Buddhism by the end of Northern Wei.

Today Pure Land Buddhism is the most popular branch of Buddhism in China, Japan, and South Korea.

During the Northern and Southern Dynasties, Buddhism was given a chance in the north to demonstrate its teachings, rituals, arts, architecture, and philosophical depth.

Buddhist monks also made tea popular in China.

The ongoing wars in northern China then drove many Buddhist monks south, resulting in the spread of Buddhism to an entirely new part of Chinese civilization.

It was there Buddhism met the competition...

Taoism becomes a religion

In part reacting to the popularity of Buddhism, southern aristocrats encouraged the growth of a Taoist movement that shared many of the same core tenets espoused by the famous Chinese philosopher Laozi.

Laozi is considered the founder of Taoism. It is not known for certain when Laozi actually lived. Some believe he was once a teacher of Confucius.

道
Tao

The Tao can't be expressed in words. I only use the word Tao so I can begin to help others understand its power.

I can tell you what it does.

The Tao created one, one created two, two created three, and three created the world as we know it.

Because Laozi lived so long ago no one is sure
what exactly the numbers one through three mean.
Over time, people had to guess at their significance.
One interpretation of Laozi's theory was:

The Tao created one
The Tao created Taiji,
a single point at which
all matter and energy
was concentrated

One created two
Taiji created Yin and Yang,
interconnected but opposing forces

Two created three
Yin and Yang created
three kinds of Qi,
the life forces of
heaven, earth,
and humans

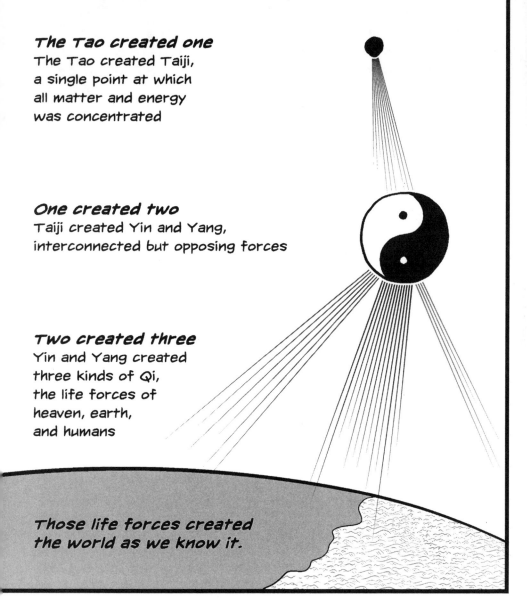

*Those life forces created
the world as we know it.*

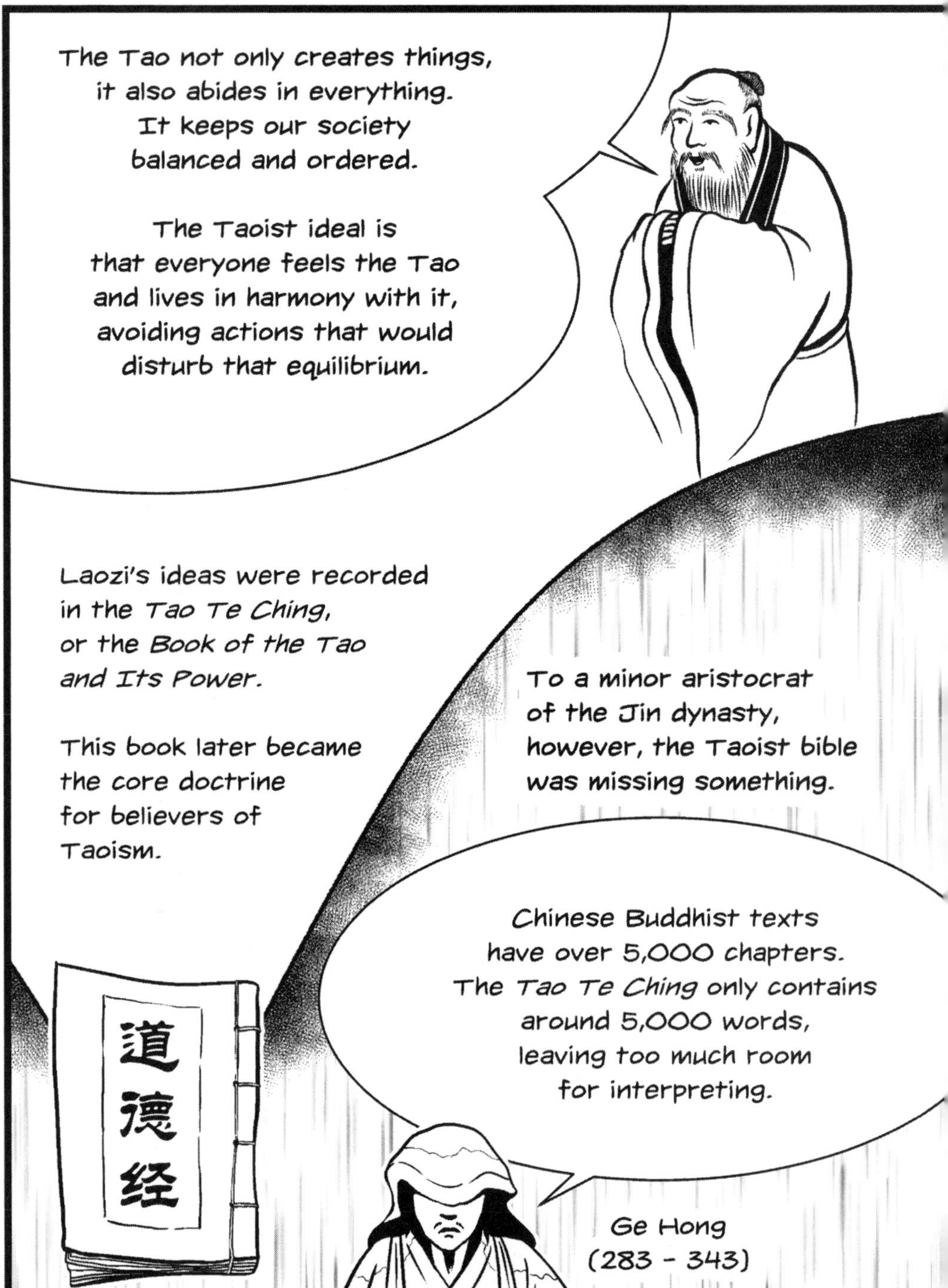
The Tao not only creates things, it also abides in everything. It keeps our society balanced and ordered.
The Taoist ideal is that everyone feels the Tao and lives in harmony with it, avoiding actions that would disturb that equilibrium.
Laozi's ideas were recorded in the *Tao Te Ching*, or the *Book of the Tao and Its Power*.
This book later became the core doctrine for believers of Taoism.
To a minor aristocrat of the Jin dynasty, however, the Taoist bible was missing something.
道德经
Chinese Buddhist texts have over 5,000 chapters. The *Tao Te Ching* only contains around 5,000 words, leaving too much room for interpreting.
Ge Hong (283 - 343)

I should gather more information to help people understand what the Tao is really about.

Ge Hong compiled various pieces of information about Chinese religion and philosophy into a massive tome of 310 chapters. 20 of those chapters were dedicated to explaining Taoism.

Philosophy
Alchemy
Meditation
Taoist yoga
Breathing exercises
Chinese medicine
Magic

Government
Politics
Law
Literature
Education

His journey to understand China's past established an important historical link for historians between early Taoist philosophy and the later Taoist religion.

Taoist practices

Ge Hong had many contemporaries who created new Taoist practices that were centered on the idea of a life force, known in Chinese as Qi.

Feng shui

Feng shui was a Chinese art that sought to gather Qi as a means to obtain good luck, health, and wealth.

The earliest discussion of feng shui was in the Taoist *Book of Burial* by Guo Pu (276 – 324).

Following the principles of feng shui, you can find the right tomb site to gather Qi from the deceased to benefit the living.

中药
Chinese medicine

气功
Qigong

针灸
Acupuncture

Qigong, an exercise to balance Qi
for healing or meditation

These topics were part of the *Yellow Emperor's Inner Canon*, a major book written about Taoist practices, and the earliest Chinese medical text. The original book was lost due to war. A scholar-physician, Huangfu Mi (215 – 282), compiled what he could save into a version that survives today.

Buddhism vs. Taoism

After Ge Hong passed away, different Taoist sects sprouted up.
These sects soon began to compete with Buddhism for followers.

During the Northern and Southern dynasties, one Taoist sect
convinced Emperor Taiwu of Northern Wei (408 - 452) to
ban Buddhism.

Destroy Buddhist religious sites
to free up resources
for Taoist temples.

The six-year period of
anti-Buddhist persecution ended
when the Taoist emperor died.

The next emperor was a Buddhist.
Buddhism returned to the north. Soon the tides
would turn and Taoists would be persecuted.

In southern China, Emperor Wu of Liang (464 – 549) viewed Taoism, Buddhism, and Confucianism as different stages of political philosophy.

In my early days, I used military power to repel invading barbarians, win a civil war, and establish the Liang dynasty.

To rule the state, first I rebuilt social order with Confucian principles.

Then, I adopted a Taoist approach, believing that the less the ruler does, the more gets done.

After the age of 50, Buddhism opened my eyes to the power of religious belief. Imagine a world where everyone has a faith. How peaceful...

Emperor Wu chose Buddhism as the state religion, with a couple of special characteristics thrown in.

Buddhists should respect their parents and devote their lives to their country.

Really? True Buddhists must cut all family and social ties if they are to pursue enlightenment.

The emperor was a vegetarian, and he ordered monks to be the same.

Since then, vegetarianism has been a feature of Chinese Buddhism.

Monks in India, Tibet, and Japan can eat meat.

Even the founder of Buddhism didn't require his followers to be vegetarian.

The balance between north and south

Emperor Wu liked going on religious retreats where he would stay in temples for extended periods of time to work and meditate. But danger awaited him back home.

I asked you to marry me into a noble family and you refused.

If I can't join you as a noble, I will make you my slaves.

Hou Jing (? – 552) was a northern warlord who had defected to the Liang.

In 548, Hou laid siege to the Liang capital and trapped Emperor Wu in the palace.

The siege lasted over six months. Out of 120,000 residents in the capital, only 2,000 survived. In the final moments of the battle, Hou Jing broke into the palace and found Emperor Wu sitting in his private chambers.

You've been fighting so long. Aren't you tired?

Suddenly, Hou couldn't talk...

He slowly turned away and left the room.

Lock him away!

A few months later, the 86-year old emperor died.

A civil war followed as Hou Jing fought to subdue other Liang generals. States in northern China took the opportunity to invade.

The Liang dynasty had prospered for four decades, longer than any dynasty during the Age of Division. Thanks to Hou Jing's thirst for power, however, that all came to an end and the Liang eventually collapsed.

In 557, a former Liang general took over what was left of the Liang and established the Chen dynasty.

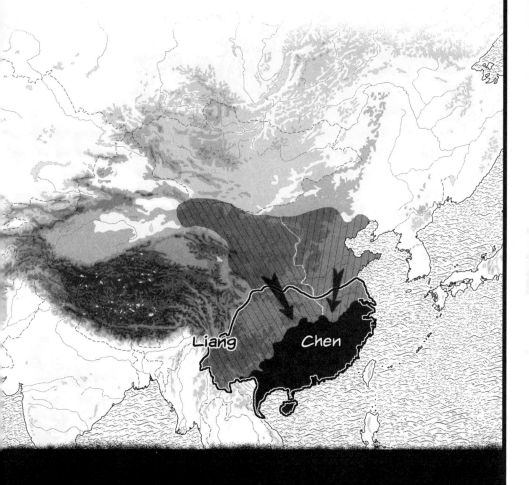

The balance of power between the north and south was broken.

THE SUI DYNASTY

589 - 618

By the end of the Age of Division,
centuries of nomadic rule had fundamentally
changed the lives of the northern Chinese.

We used to sit on the floor.
Now we sit on chairs.

We used to wear sandals
and slippers. Now we wear
shoes and boots.

We used to wear long
and loose robes. Now we wear
shorter and tighter clothes.

We used to think
thin women were beautiful.
Now we think full-bodied
women are beautiful.

For generations, the Xianbei and other nomad tribes had intermarried with the local Han population in northern China.

Eventually, different ethnic groups like the Xianbei began to identify as Han Chinese.

Today, Han Chinese account for 92% of China's population, or 20% of the world's population. It is the single largest ethnic group on earth.

In 581, Emperor Wen (541 – 604) founded the Sui dynasty in northern China.

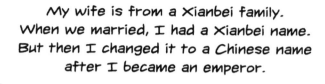

My wife is from a Xianbei family.
When we married, I had a Xianbei name.
But then I changed it to a Chinese name
after I became an emperor.

To defend the new state without bankrupting the economy,
I will enforce the equal-field system practiced
by northern dynasties.

In this system, the government owns the land and
assigns it to families. In return, people pay taxes or
offer to serve as members of the militia.

Land

By 588, the Sui had amassed an army of 518,000.
The Chen dynasty in the south had no way to resist and
was conquered by the Sui.

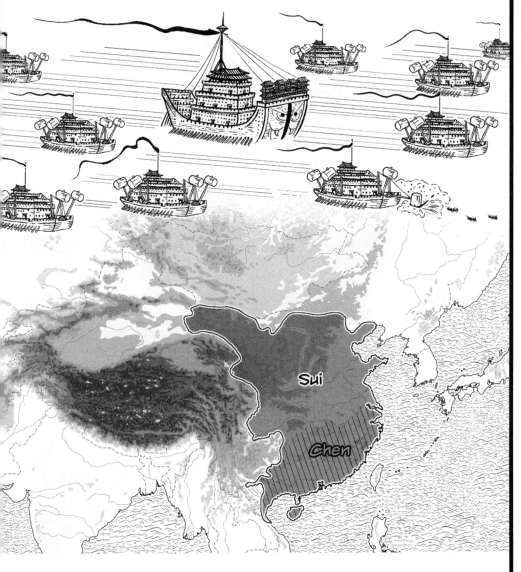

In 589, after nearly 400 years of fragmentation,
China was unified under the Sui dynasty.

Improved governance and national projects

To centralize control over its vast empire, the Sui improved the systems of governance used by previous Chinese dynasties.

The imperial examination system

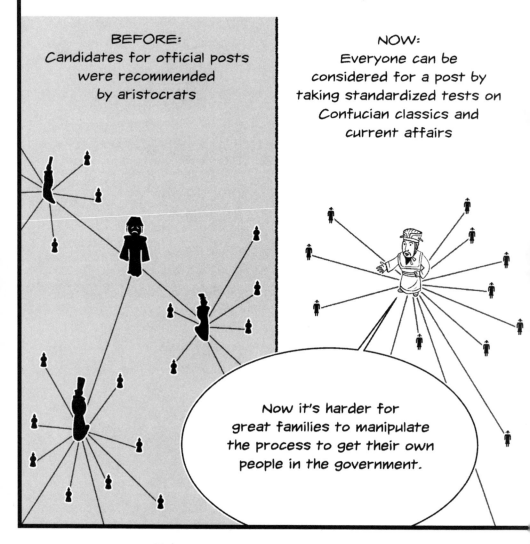

BEFORE:
Candidates for official posts were recommended by aristocrats

NOW:
Everyone can be considered for a post by taking standardized tests on Confucian classics and current affairs

Now it's harder for great families to manipulate the process to get their own people in the government.

The three departments and six ministries
(the central government)

BEFORE:
1 chancellor was responsible for running the central government

Rites   Palace guards

Security   Horses

Justice   State visits

Imperial clan

Agriculture   Treasurer

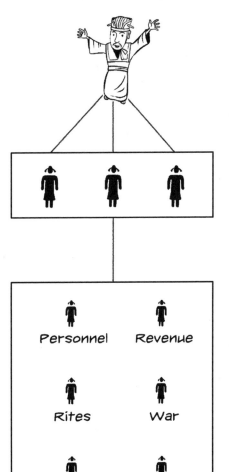

NOW:
3 chancellors are responsible for government affairs and check each other's power

Personnel   Revenue

Rites   War

Justice   Works

The Sui transformed China's landscape with huge projects.

Rebuilt the Great Wall to defend against nomads in the north

Established a new capital city in Chang'an

Built a second capital at Luoyang

Created national granaries with enough food to feed the whole country for 50 years

Constructed the Grand Canal*

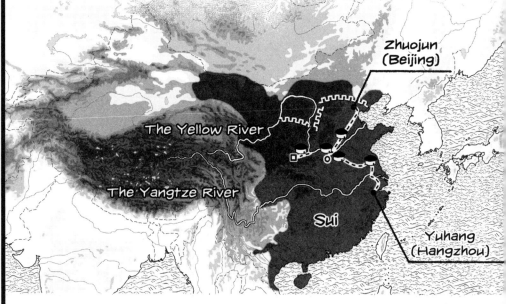

Zhuojun (Beijing)

The Yellow River

The Yangtze River

Sui

Yuhang (Hangzhou)

* The Grand Canal was about 1,200 miles long. It was the longest artificial river ever built and took 5 million workers five years to complete. Its main function was to supply food for the two capitals and troops in northern China.

A "small" problem shatters the Sui

From its initial founding, the Sui had to defend against
military incursions and raids from all directions.
While the Sui was mostly able to secure its borders,
the Goguryeo kingdom in modern-day Korea still threatened.

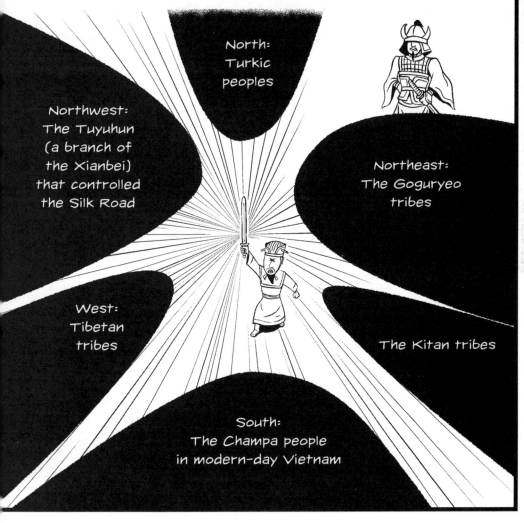

North:
Turkic
peoples

Northwest:
The Tuyuhun
(a branch of
the Xianbei)
that controlled
the Silk Road

Northeast:
The Goguryeo
tribes

West:
Tibetan
tribes

The Kitan tribes

South:
The Champa people
in modern-day Vietnam

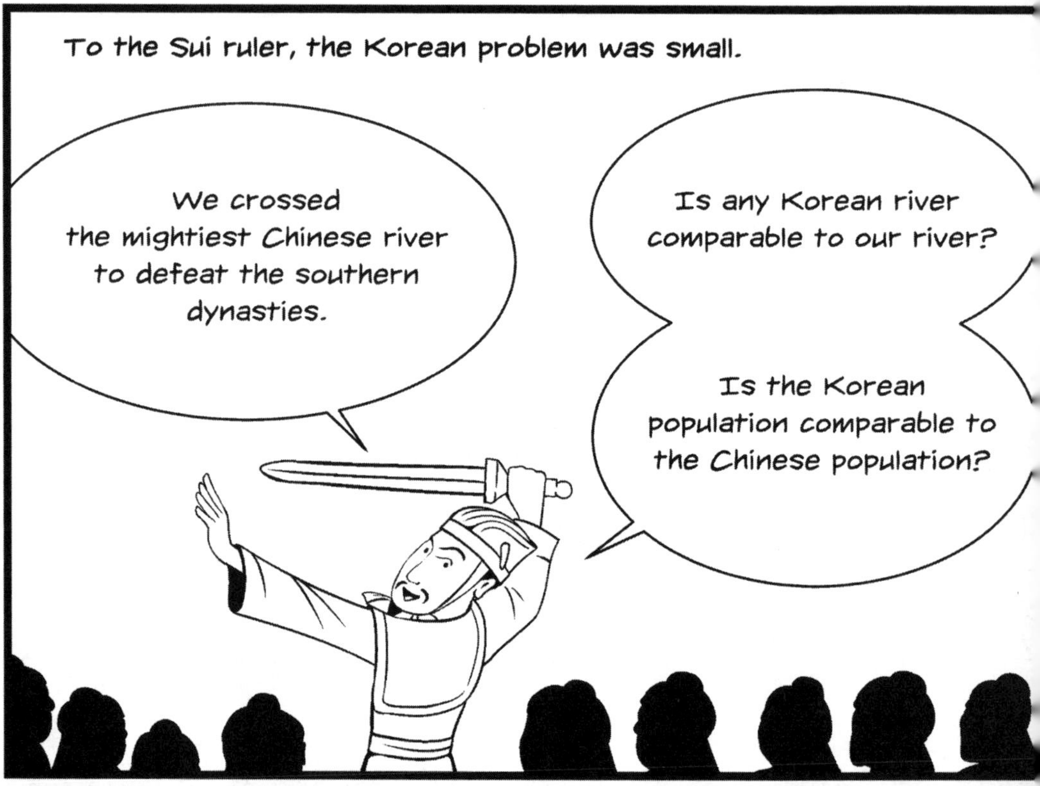
To the Sui ruler, the Korean problem was small.
We crossed the mightiest Chinese river to defeat the southern dynasties.
Is any Korean river comparable to our river?
Is the Korean population comparable to the Chinese population?

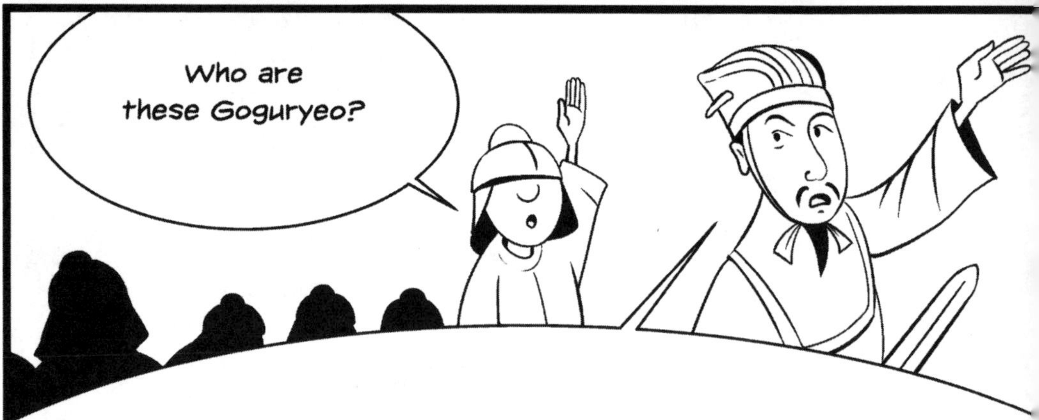
Who are these Goguryeo?
The Han dynasty once controlled a part of northeast Asia. However, some local groups banded together to resist the Han. These locals went on to form the Goguryeo kingdom.

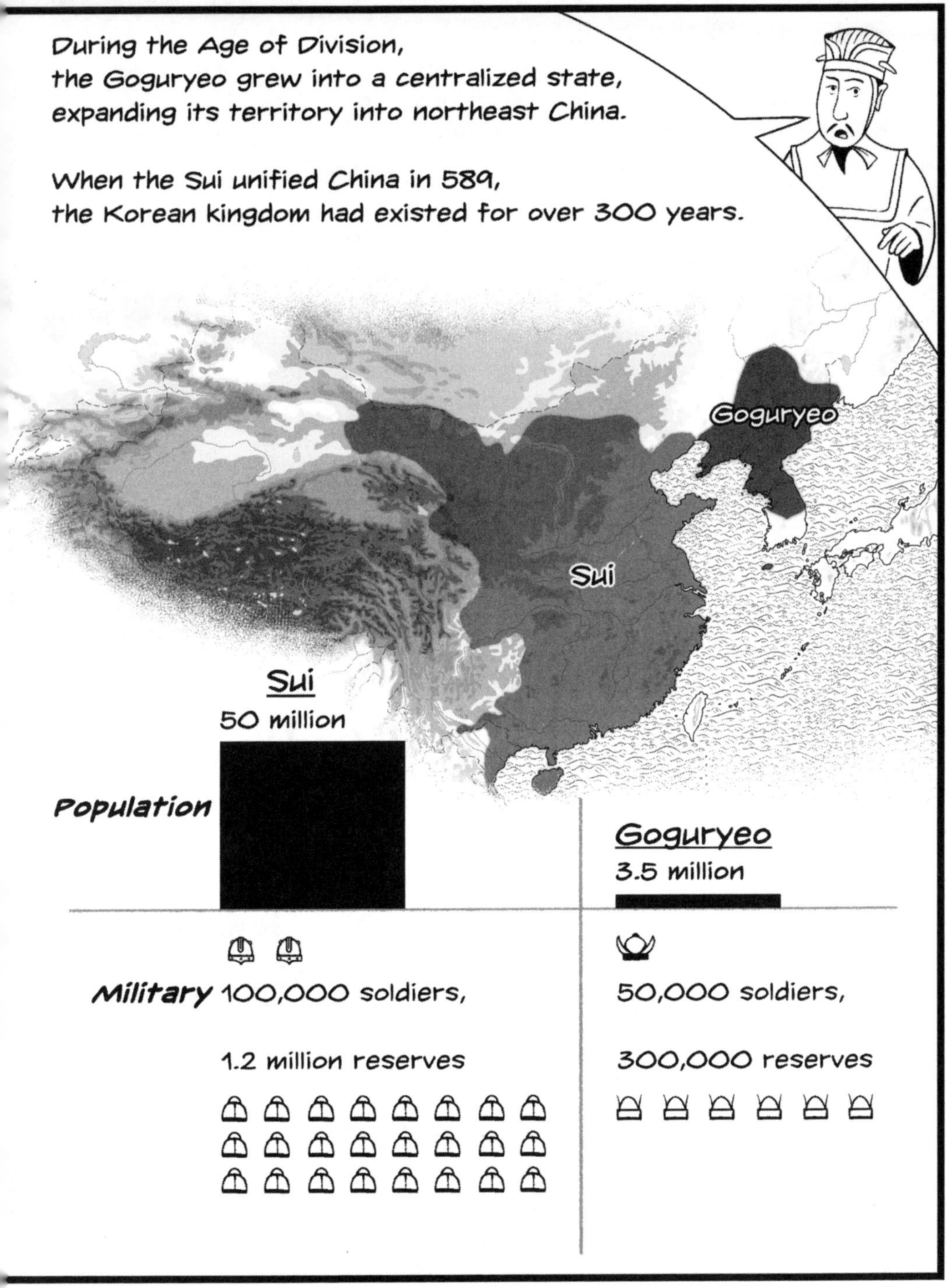
During the Age of Division,
the Goguryeo grew into a centralized state,
expanding its territory into northeast China.
When the Sui unified China in 589,
the Korean kingdom had existed for over 300 years.
Goguryeo
Sui
Population
Sui
50 million
Goguryeo
3.5 million
Military
100,000 soldiers,
1.2 million reserves
50,000 soldiers,
300,000 reserves

While the Sui was reinforcing troops in northeast Asia, the Goguryeo allied with other tribes and carried out border raids on the Sui.

In 598, I sent 300,000 troops to attack the Goguryeo.

After a combination of bad weather, disease, and enemy ambushes, we met total defeat and suffered 90% casualties.

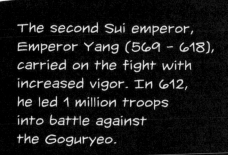

The second Sui emperor, Emperor Yang (569 – 618), carried on the fight with increased vigor. In 612, he led 1 million troops into battle against the Goguryeo.

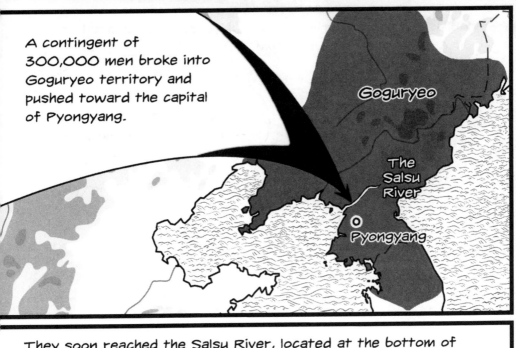

A contingent of 300,000 men broke into Goguryeo territory and pushed toward the capital of Pyongyang.

They soon reached the Salsu River, located at the bottom of a wide, flat valley.

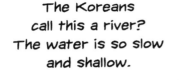

The Koreans call this a river? The water is so slow and shallow.

We can cross it by foot in only an hour. It's muddy, walk carefully.

No Sui soldier would have imagined this small puddle might bring about his end.

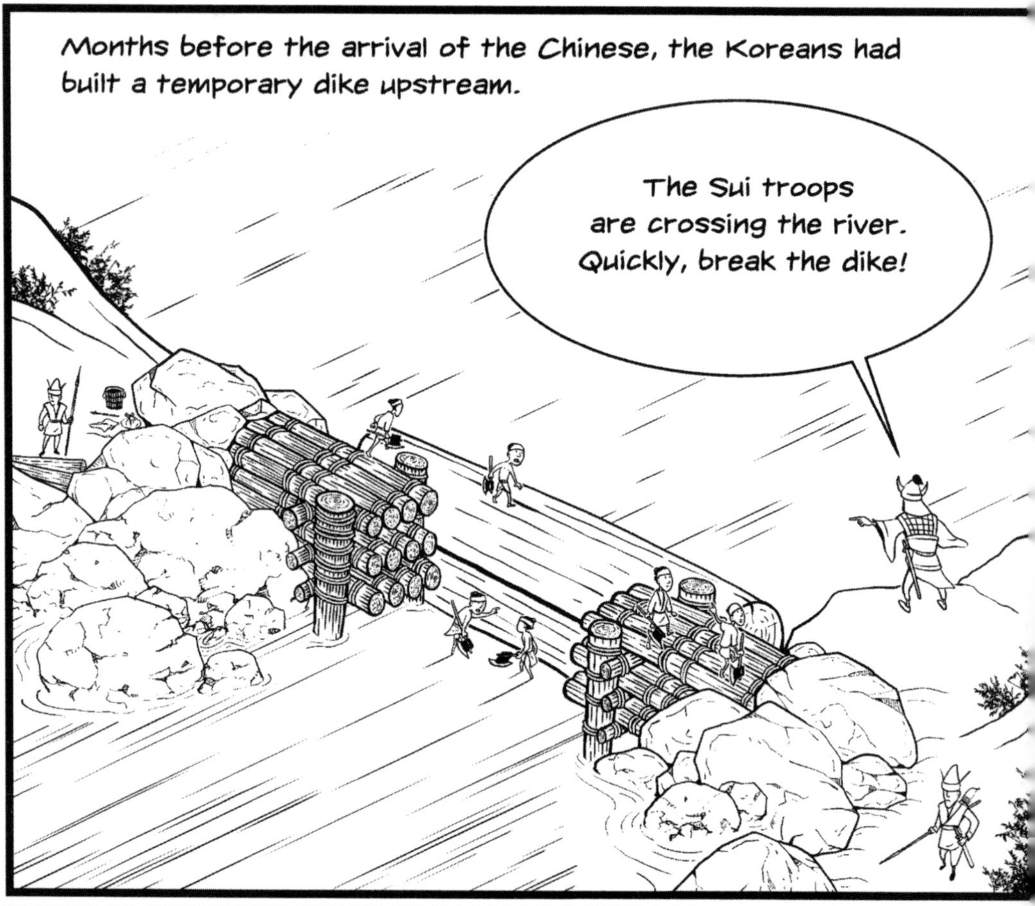
Months before the arrival of the Chinese, the Koreans had built a temporary dike upstream.
The Sui troops are crossing the river. Quickly, break the dike!

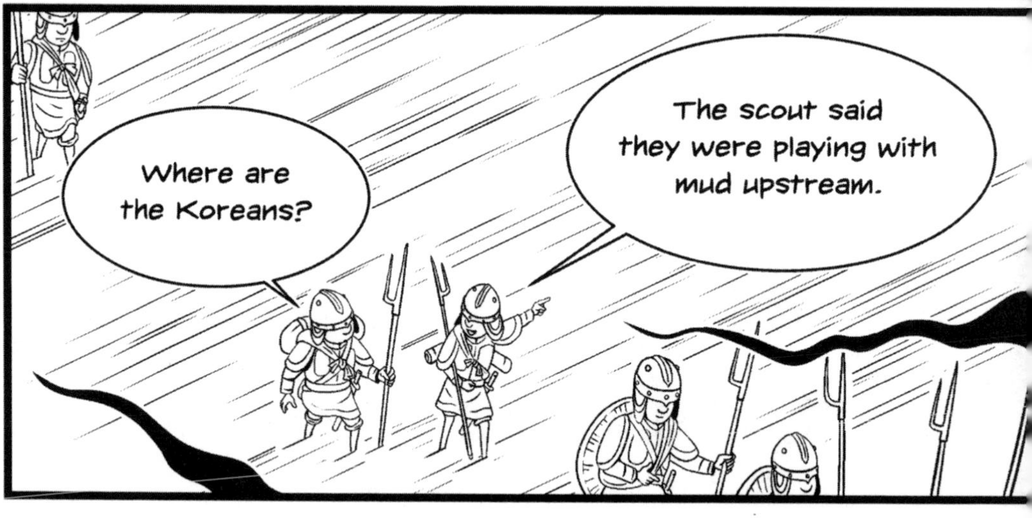
Where are the Koreans?
The scout said they were playing with mud upstream.

The water rose
steadily.

The fully equipped Sui soldiers could no longer keep their balance.
Men in tight formation started to trip, fall down, and get stuck.

By the time they realized what was happening, the soldiers
in the water could not reach either bank. Panic ensued.

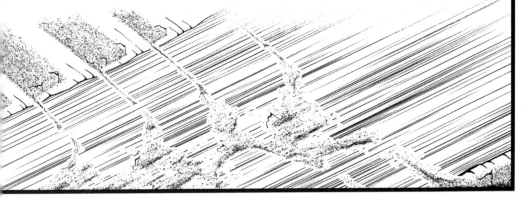

At that moment the Korean cavalry charged.
The Chinese who had crossed the river were cut down like grass.
Stuck in the mud, they were easy targets for Korean archers.
The surviving Sui soldiers retreated, suffering ambush
after ambush as they fled.

Of the initial 300,000 men that embarked to
fight the Goguryeo, only 2,700 made it back to China.

But Emperor Yang wouldn't give up. In 613, he was again preparing to attack the Goguryeo. However, unrest at home prevented him from launching an assault.

Your Majesty, our Sui generals have rebelled. They have cut off our supply of food and attacked the capital. Some have even defected to the Koreans.

After crushing most of the rebellion, Emperor Yang attempted a last invasion in 614, even as unrest in China continued.

Your Majesty, there are still revolts all over China!

Empire collapses

Endless problems overwhelmed Emperor Yang.

> Honor and dishonor,
> wealth and poverty,
> as well as pain and pleasure
> all come in cycles.
> Let's just be happy.

Our army suffered
millions of deaths in Korea,
followed by rebellions
across China.
It's all your fault!

Imperial Guard

Kill him!

I admit that
I failed my people,
but I didn't fail you.

I gave you
so much power
and wealth.

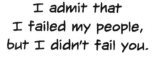

You are my guards
and I trusted my life
to you.

Not sure what to say, one officer killed Emperor Yang's youngest son.

If you want me dead, find me poison and I will take my own life.

I don't know where to find it.

Then think of some other way...

Emperor Yang's cousin, Li Yuan (566 – 635), efficiently took control of the Sui capital and established the Tang dynasty.

20 different rebel groups challenged the newly established Tang. It took 10 years for the Tang to defeat its opponents and reunify China.

THE TANG DYNASTY

618 – 907

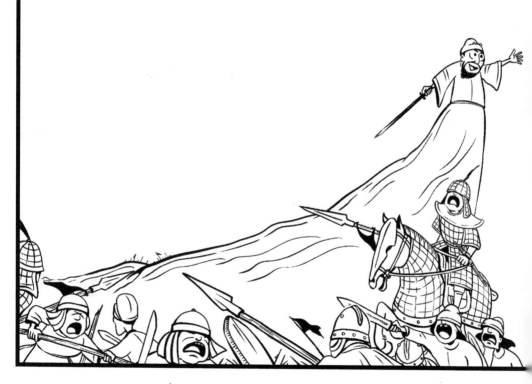

The Tang inherited many things from the Sui dynasty:

✓ The equal-field system

✓ The three departments and six ministries

✓ Imperial examinations

✓ The Grand Canal

✓ Sui granaries

✓ Fewer and weaker nomads due to military campaigns led by the Sui rulers

All in all, the Tang were off to a good start.

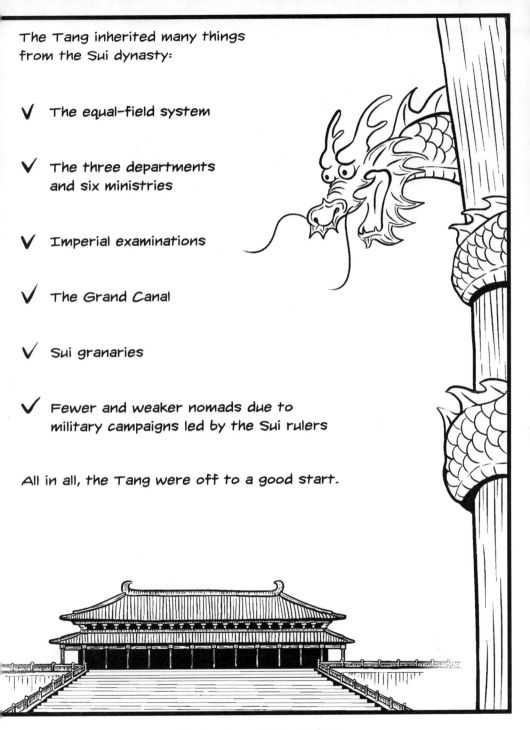

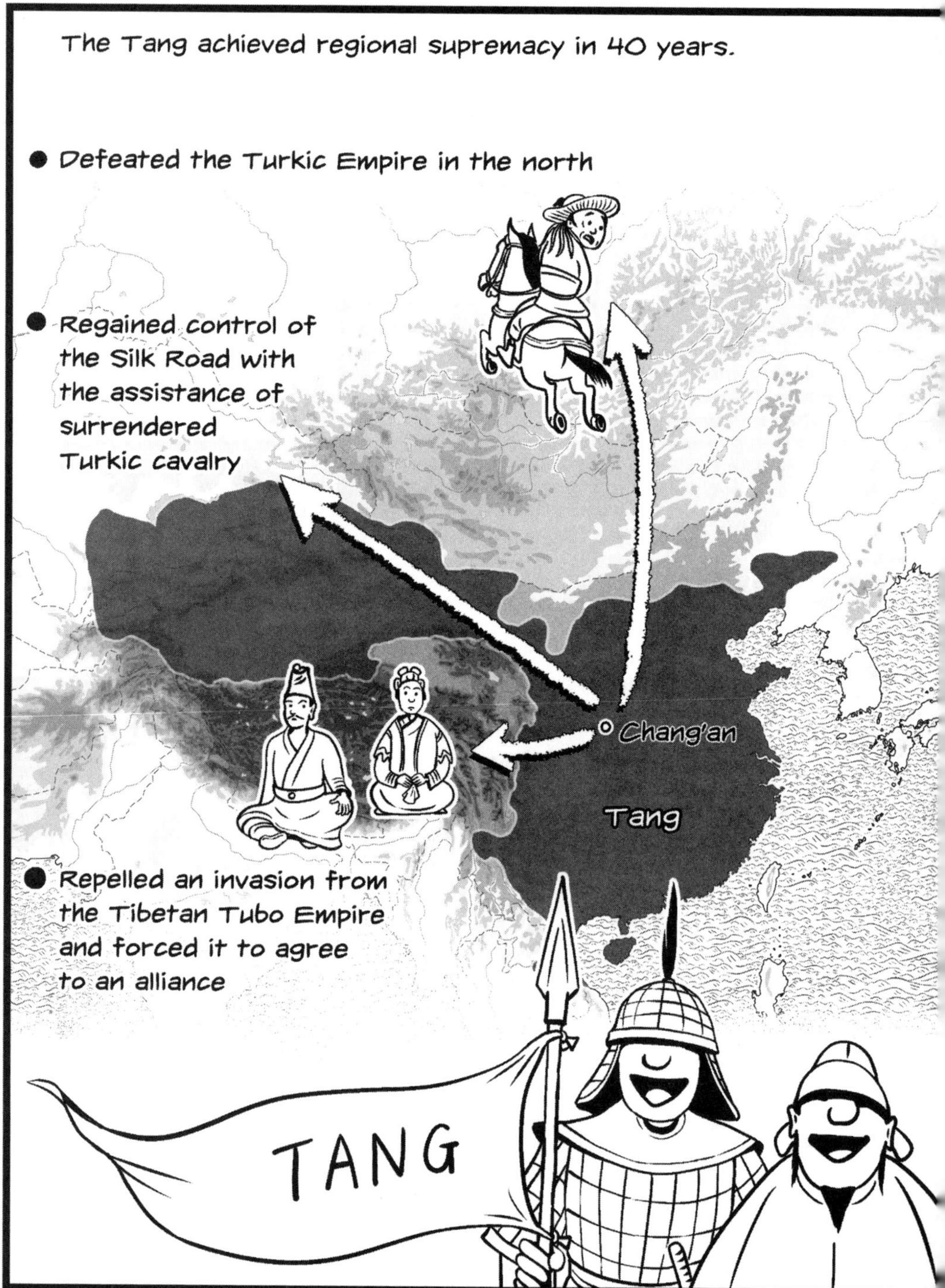
The Tang achieved regional supremacy in 40 years.
Defeated the Turkic Empire in the north
Regained control of the Silk Road with the assistance of surrendered Turkic cavalry
Chang'an
Tang
Repelled an invasion from the Tibetan Tubo Empire and forced it to agree to an alliance
TANG

The Tang dynasty established its own world order.

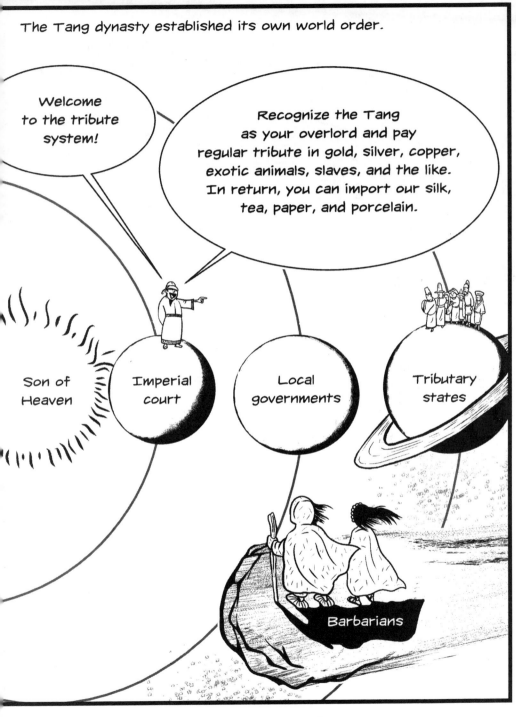

Arabs, Persians, Jews, Turks, Indians, Japanese, Koreans, and Southeast Asians came to China to do business and study.

Guangzhou ⇌ The Red Sea

Foreigners brought in new religions such as Islam, Nestorian Christianity, and Judaism, adding to a cultural diversity perhaps unmatched in the history of China.

The imperial capital, Chang'an, became an international center of trade and culture.

In Chinese history textbooks today, the Tang dynasty is considered China's golden age.

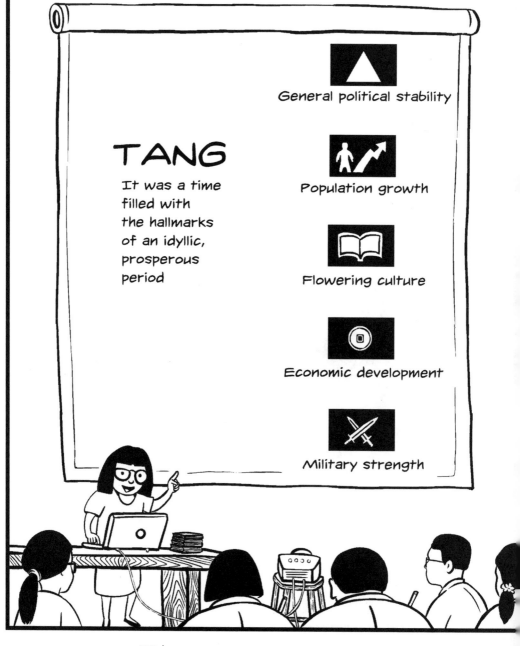

TANG

It was a time filled with the hallmarks of an idyllic, prosperous period

General political stability

Population growth

Flowering culture

Economic development

Military strength

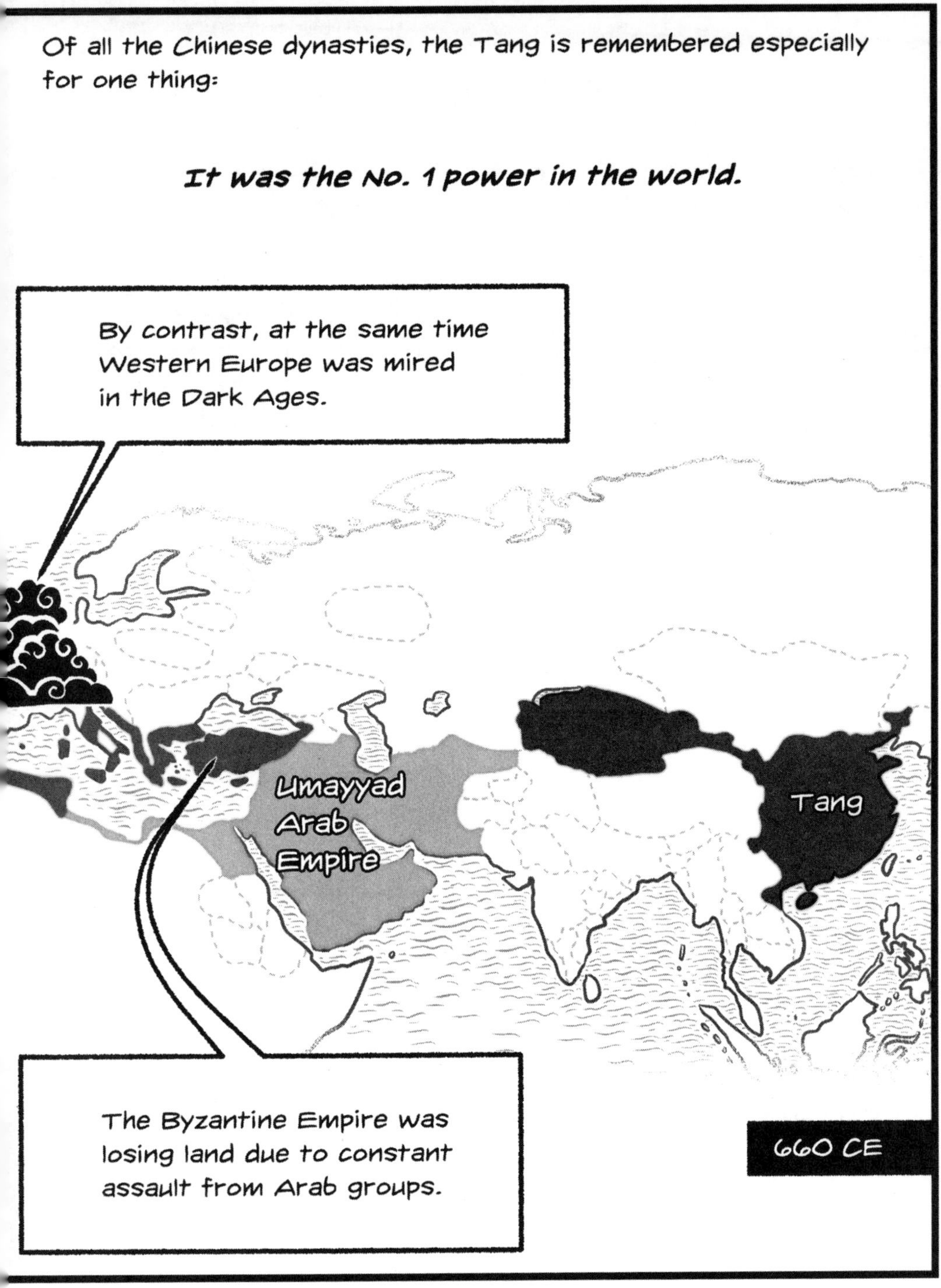
Of all the Chinese dynasties, the Tang is remembered especially for one thing:
It was the No. 1 power in the world.
By contrast, at the same time Western Europe was mired in the Dark Ages.
Umayyad Arab Empire
Tang
The Byzantine Empire was losing land due to constant assault from Arab groups.
660 CE

Life in a golden age

To ordinary people in the early Tang, life wasn't all that glorious, especially for the 80% living in the countryside.

The urban-rural gap was wide!

Farmers were granted a share of land by the state. In return, they paid taxes with grain, cloth, and labor. They weren't allowed to move once they were allocated land.

In cities, the gentry held 95% of the official posts and they operated a wide range of profitable businesses: textiles, porcelain, wine, tea, sugar, salt, iron, shipbuilding, import and export...

Women from rich families could attend school, compose poetry, and play polo.

Peasant women worked at least as hard as men. They had to raise children, work in the fields, and weave textiles.

The wealthy had ice pits to keep food.

The farmers could only afford salt to preserve their food.

I hire laborers to carve blocks of ice from frozen lakes in mountains so my family can enjoy chilled fruit on hot summer days.

Dad, why do we eat pickles every day?

Inequality was reinforced by law. Different social ranks were represented by eight colors.

purple **dark red**
light red **dark green**
light green **dark blue**
light blue
yellow

Peasants must dress in yellow with very few accessories.

The most senior officials dressed in purple and wore jewelry of their choice.

Challenges to political stability

The successes of the early Tang weren't able to heal the deep fractures in society left by the Age of Division. Underneath lurked challenges to the throne posed by regional aristocracies. Each faction had its representatives in court.

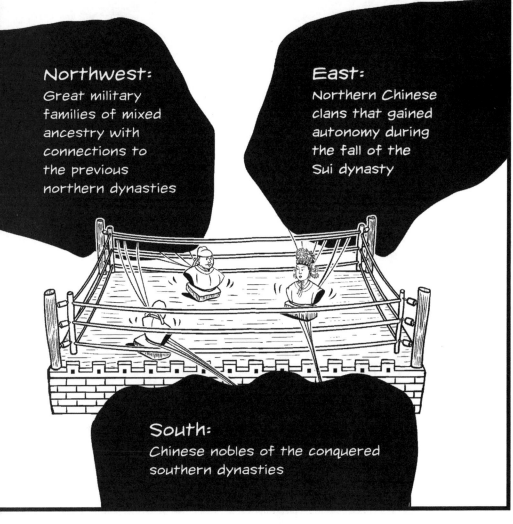

Northwest:
Great military families of mixed ancestry with connections to the previous northern dynasties

East:
Northern Chinese clans that gained autonomy during the fall of the Sui dynasty

South:
Chinese nobles of the conquered southern dynasties

The imperial family tried to balance the interests of these different groups, but often failed.

Li Shimin (598 – 649), later Emperor Taizong of Tang

Supported by military aristocracy in the northwest

My brother is the crown prince and many Chinese clans think he should be the next emperor.

Li killed his 2 brothers and their 10 young sons to seize the throne from his father.

Wu Zetian (624 – 705), the only female emperor in Chinese history

Supported by the Chinese clans in the east and south

I want to move the capital to Luoyang, closer to the regional powers on my side.

She killed 2 of her sons and deposed another 2 to fend off the military families in the northwest.

Emperor Xuanzong (685 – 762) ruled for 43 years, the longest reign of the Tang

Supported by the aristocrats in the northwest

To secure his position, Xuanzong killed 2 of his aunts and a cousin.

First female emperor

The story of Wu Zetian is still popular in China today.

Wu was Emperor Taizong's concubine. After Taizong died, Wu won the heart of his son, Emperor Gaozong (628 – 683).

Gaozong had health problems and he asked Wu Zetian to help him with his work ruling the country.

When Gaozong passed away, Wu was prepared to be the de facto ruler.

Many Tang loyalists opposed Wu Zetian.

She slept with a father and a son. How can such a woman rule a state?

Wu hit the opposition hard. Her secret police carried out systematic torture and executions.

In addition to violence, she also needed something "softer" to justify her rule.

Most imperial family members are Taoists and the government is full of Confucian officials, many of them trying to get rid of me.

Don't they know neither Confucian nor Taoist classics say a woman can't be a ruler?

Who needs them?! I'll get support from the people by adopting their religion, Buddhism.

Buddhism was widely popular before Wu Zetian rose to power.
The passion people had for it was best displayed by
Chinese monk Xuanzang (602 – 664).

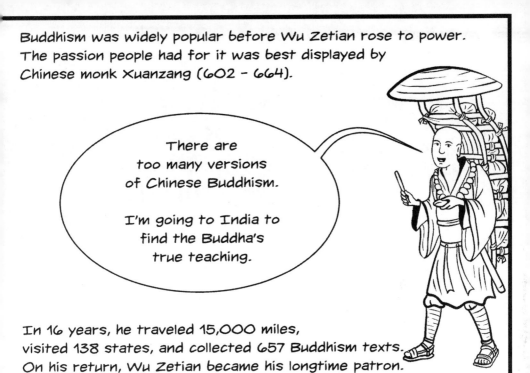

There are
too many versions
of Chinese Buddhism.

I'm going to India to
find the Buddha's
true teaching.

In 16 years, he traveled 15,000 miles,
visited 138 states, and collected 657 Buddhism texts.
On his return, Wu Zetian became his longtime patron.

Xuanzang's adventure inspired a Ming-dynasty novel.

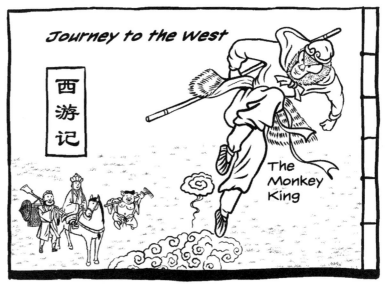

Journey to the West

西游记

The Monkey King

At age 65, Wu Zetian took the throne from her son and declared the Zhou dynasty (690 – 705).

To boost the image of her Buddhist country, Wu gave Buddhist temples great economic and social power.

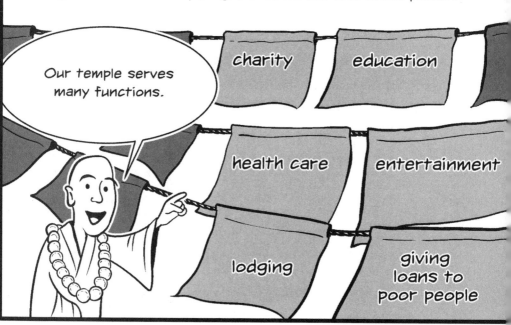

To standardize Buddhist texts, her government sponsored massive printing projects.

We carve text and images into wooden blocks. We then press paper on those blocks to make books.

The earliest surviving book printed on wooden blocks dates to Wu Zetian's reign.

With Wu Zetian's support, China became the center of Buddhism, attracting students, scholars, and pilgrims from all over Asia.

Around that time, Buddhism was fading in India. One major Indian Buddhist kingdom disintegrated into small warring states. Indian Buddhist monks were persecuted in several regions and many escaped to China.

Chan Buddhism

Buddhist masters were more than happy to accept Wu Zetian's patronage, with the exception of one monk.
This monk practiced a branch of Buddhism called Chan.

Huineng (638 – 713) was the sixth and last patriarch of Chan Buddhism

Wu Zetian sent an official to Huineng's temple.

Please come with me to the capital. Your visit will enlighten the hearts of countless people, and ease their suffering.

People fear suffering, and try to avoid it.

Fear fills their hearts, clouds their decisions, and eventually defines who they are.

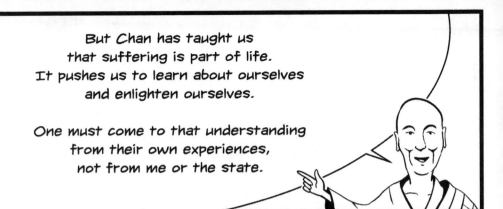

But Chan has taught us that suffering is part of life. It pushes us to learn about ourselves and enlighten ourselves.

One must come to that understanding from their own experiences, not from me or the state.

The official went back and reported everything to Wu Zetian.

Who is this man?

According to legend, Huineng came from a poor family and once was a kitchen worker at East Mountain Temple...

One day in 661, the fifth Chan patriarch was about to select his successor.

Students, please write down your understanding of Chan Buddhism. The winner will be the next patriarch.

Hongren
(601 – 674)

His top student wrote a poem on the wall. Everyone was impressed.

The body is the tree of enlightenment,
The mind is a mirror,
Polish them at all times,
So no dust can settle.

Huineng overheard their conversation. After everyone was gone, he went to the wall.

Huineng stopped a scholar passing by.

Sir, could you help me write down my idea? I can't write...

What could you possibly know about Chan?

With all due respect, sir, whether one is illiterate or a scholar has nothing to do with Chan enlightenment.

Huineng's poem created a big stir.

Enlightenment is not a tree,
Nor the mind a mirror,
Look beyond all illusions,
Where can dust actually settle?

His young mind is so original and so pure, free from any attachment. He sees the fundamental truth better than anyone else.

I would like to pass my duties on to such a person.

But he is illiterate.

After I die, my students will be jealous and will try to harm him.

The wise master made a difficult choice. He took Huineng to his secret chamber.

Please accept my robe and bowl, they are the symbols of my title that I pass to you.

Tonight you must go as far away as possible and continue the teaching of Chan.

Everything of the material world
is temporary, oppressive, and illusory.

To achieve enlightenment,
you don't have to read, write,
go to a temple, or travel to India.
The path to enlightenment is simply in your heart
and is beyond logic and reasoning.

When meditating don't set any goals.
Just watch the stream of your thoughts
without interfering.

Wu Zetian was moved by Huineng's life story.

The country is lucky
to have a man like Huineng.

Please ask him to accept my respect.
Renovate his home and build him
a temple to show my appreciation.

Tang restoration

In 705, Wu Zetian turned 80 and fell ill.
Her officials staged a coup to remove her
from power and reestablish the Tang.
She died in the same year
under heavy guard.

The restored Tang dynasty continued to grow.
Under the reign of Emperor Xuanzong,
the Tang reached its peak in terms
of economic, cultural,
and military strength.
Its population exploded.

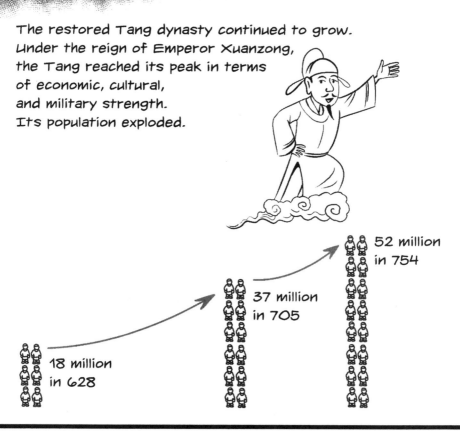

52 million
in 754

37 million
in 705

18 million
in 628

Emperor Xuanzong was a cultivated man. He composed music, played several instruments, and owned a troop of dancing horses. In his palace, there were 10,000 full-time artists, musicians, and entertainers.

His favorite concubine, Consort Yang (719 – 756), was a great singer, dancer, composer, musician, and poet.

Xuanzong established an academy for poets that attracted artists like Li Bai and Du Fu, the two greatest Chinese poets of all time.

Today, the 49,403 poems surviving from the Tang constitute nearly half of all extant Chinese classical poems. In China even kindergarteners are taught to recite them.

Li Bai
(701 - 762)

Du Fu
(712 - 770)

The sun sets behind a mountain,
The Yellow River flows to the sea;
To see beyond what the eyes can see,
We must rise to a level above.

An Lushan rebellion

While everything seemed to be going well for the Tang, Xuanzong had a pressing matter to deal with that would have big consequences.

> The state used to give land to families in exchange for their military service.
>
> When we ran out of land to give away because of overpopulation, I authorized local governors to use state funds to hire soldiers.

> In 742, the Tang built a standing army of 500,000 men. This was the first large full-time army in Chinese history.

> But governors hire soldiers loyal to them, not the state. Now the governors have their own armies. If they turn against us, we're in trouble.

Tension escalated between the court and governors and in 755 a Tang governor rebelled. His veteran army of 164,000 soldiers quickly closed in on the Tang capital.

An Lushan (703 – 757)

Fanyang (Beijing)

Chang'an

Tang

Emperor Xuanzong and his inner circle fled west.

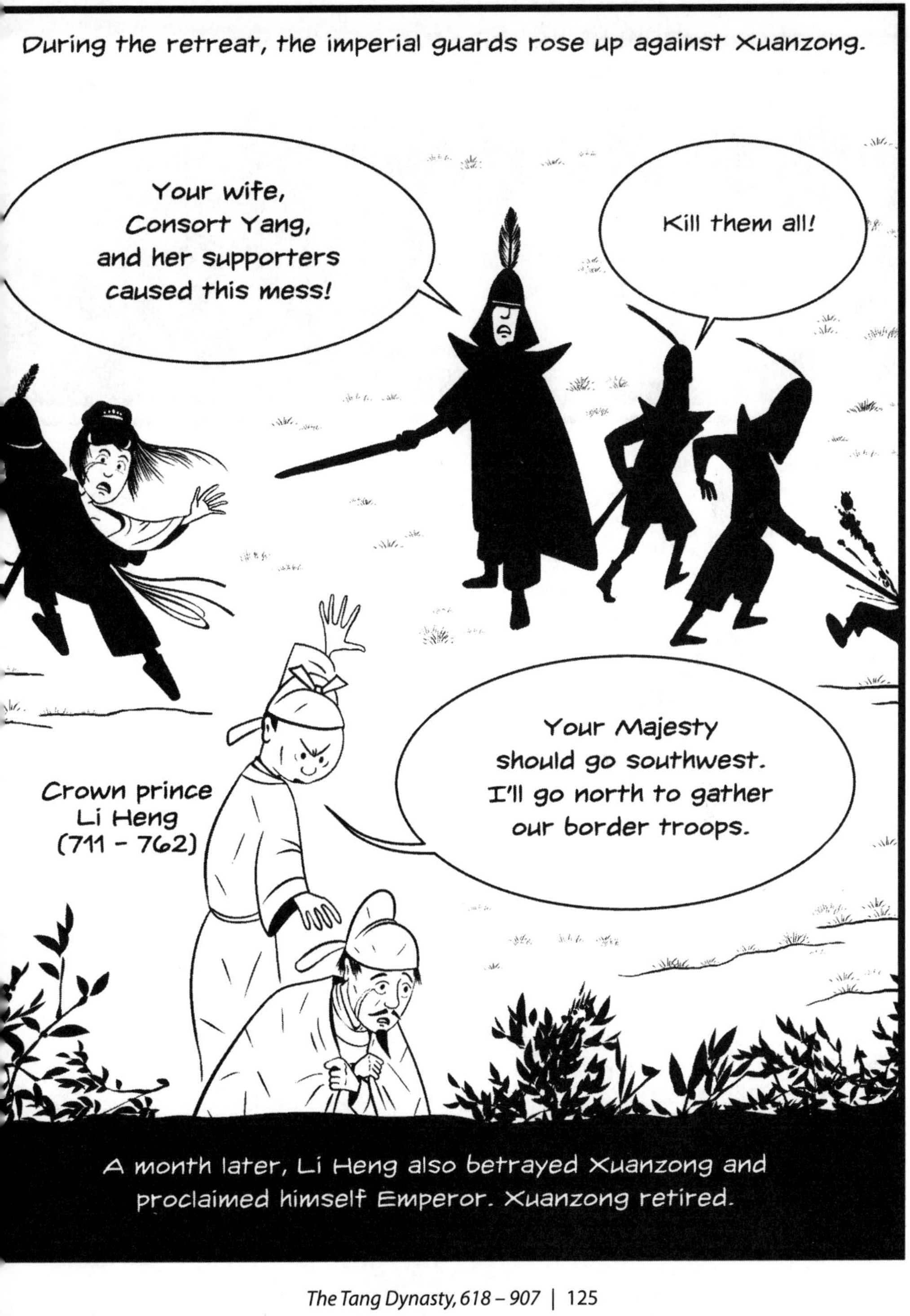
During the retreat, the imperial guards rose up against Xuanzong.
Your wife, Consort Yang, and her supporters caused this mess!
Kill them all!
Crown prince Li Heng (711 - 762)
Your Majesty should go southwest. I'll go north to gather our border troops.
A month later, Li Heng also betrayed Xuanzong and proclaimed himself Emperor. Xuanzong retired.

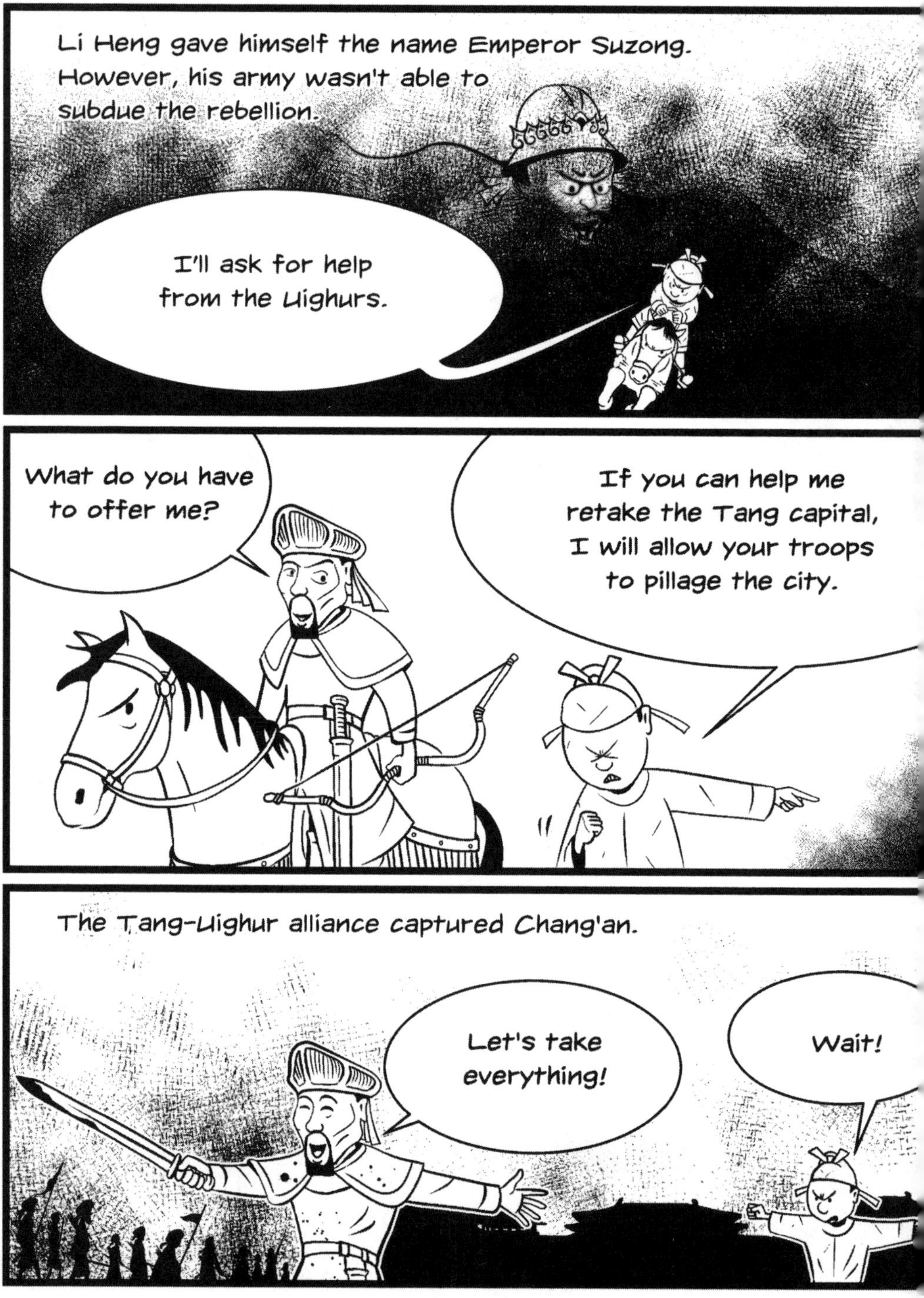
Li Heng gave himself the name Emperor Suzong. However, his army wasn't able to subdue the rebellion.
I'll ask for help from the Uighurs.
What do you have to offer me?
If you can help me retake the Tang capital, I will allow your troops to pillage the city.
The Tang-Uighur alliance captured Chang'an.
Let's take everything!
Wait!

A promise is a promise.

Luoyang is the rebel capital. If you rob Chang'an now, the people of Luoyang will oppose us at all costs!

Please leave Chang'an alone and rob Luoyang instead.

Ok, we'll rob Luoyang instead!

The rebellion took 36 million lives and lasted eight years before finally being quashed.

Decentralized power

The An Lushan rebellion forever changed the political landscape of Tang China.

After helping the Tang court crush An Lushan, many governors gained autonomy from the central government.

The most powerful governors had over 90,000 soldiers and 10,000 cavalry.

More minor ones might have 15,000 men and no cavalry.

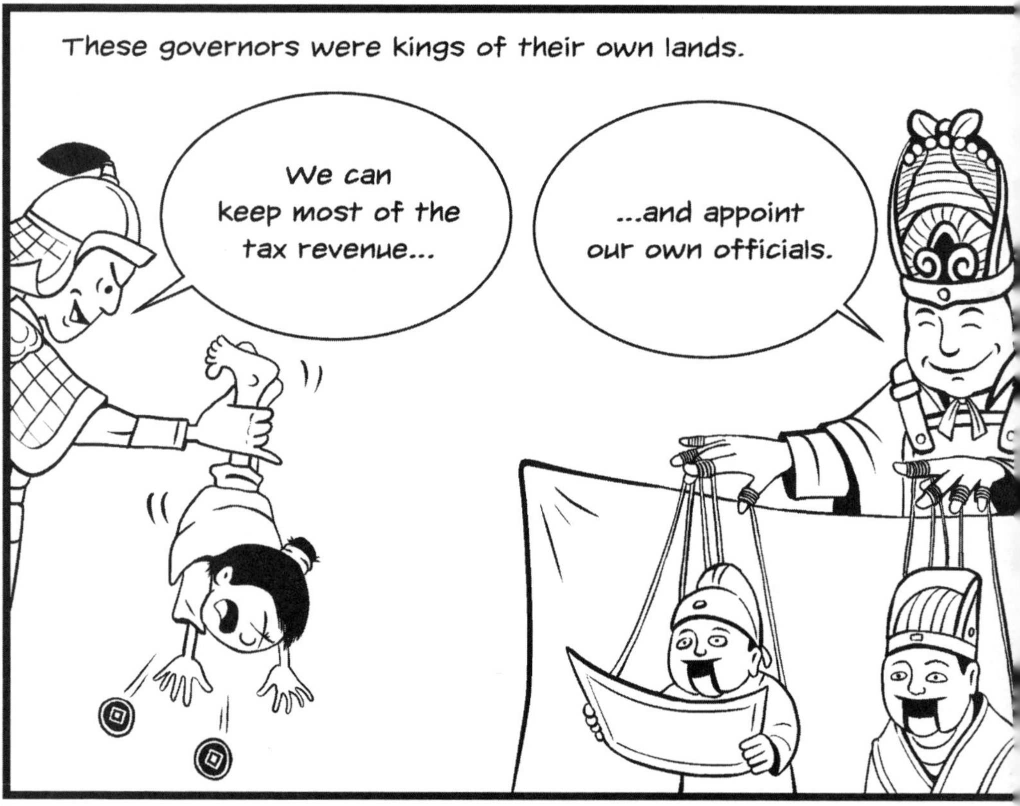
These governors were kings of their own lands.
We can keep most of the tax revenue...
...and appoint our own officials.

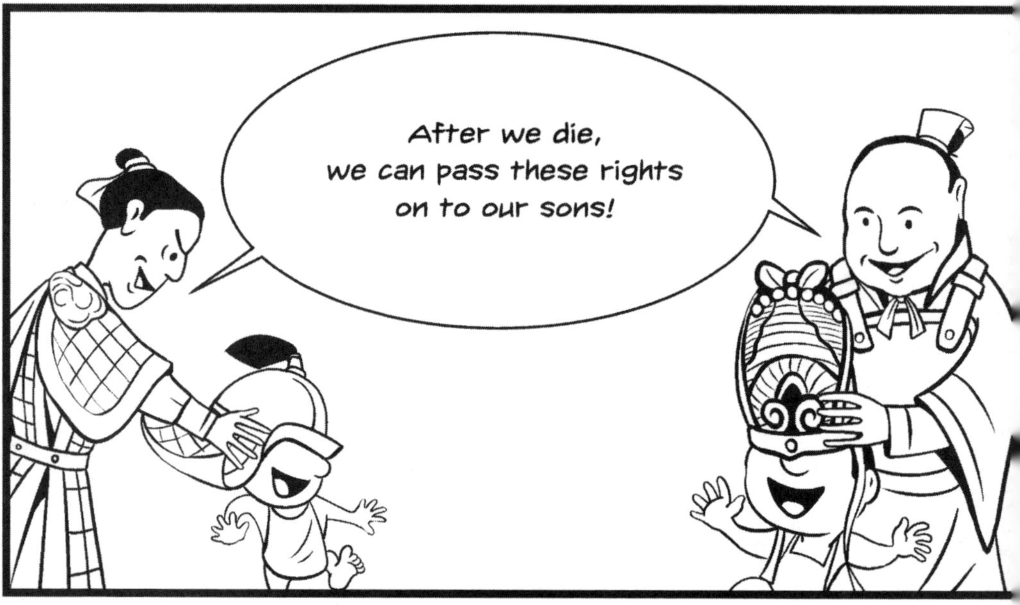
After we die, we can pass these rights on to our sons!

The Tang court withdrew from regional economies and politics. This had unintended benefits for local development.

Emperor Daizong (727 – 779), Suzong's successor, tried to save the Tang from falling apart.

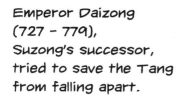

Build a central army to subdue the local governors.

Appoint my personal eunuchs as commanders.

Once in power, the eunuchs were just as hard to control as the governors.

After Daizong, the eunuch faction amassed so much political influence that they deposed one emperor, murdered two, and were firmly in control of the rest.

Buddha's money

Infighting at the court and secessionism in the provinces bankrupted the empire.

The Tang Dynasty, 618 – 907 | 133

In 844, Wuzong moved against Buddhism.

Close all Buddhist temples, take their property, and send the monks and nuns home.

44,600 Buddhist sites were destroyed, with 260,500 monks and nuns forced to vacate. This purge was by far the heaviest blow against Buddhism in China's history and marked a steep decline in its popularity.

"My flower shall slay all other flowers"

The late Tang remained weak and divided.
When a series of natural disasters and famine struck in 859,
the country fell into decades of non-stop violence.
The worst of it was led by a salt smuggler named
Huang Chao (? – 884).

I tried to become an official
by taking the imperial exams.
After failing repeatedly,
I composed a poetic curse.

Wait till autumn comes this September 8th,

My flower shall slay all other flowers,

Its billowing scent shall infiltrate Chang'an,

And the capital shall be filled with
soldiers in golden armor.

Huang's curse came true. In 881, his rebel army broke into Chang'an. Bitter street fighting engulfed the capital as Huang threatened to take control of the city.

But the tide turned against Huang when a rebel general switched sides.

The Tang promised me a big reward!

Zhu Wen (852 – 912)

Retreat!

Suffering defeat after defeat,
Huang Chao took his own life in 884.

Compared with the rebellion that brought down
the Han dynasty, the Huang Chao rebellion was
bigger, lasted longer, and completely destroyed
the Chinese aristocracy.

HAN	TANG
Yellow Turban rebellion:	Huang Chao rebellion:
6 months	**10 years**
(184)	(874 – 884)

While the rebels destroyed the great families out of hatred for their injustices, they did little to change the system itself. Eventually, the rebels became as corrupt as the people they sought to replace.

With the destruction of the nobles went their political privileges, elegant lifestyles, and family records. An aristocratic class that had existed for 1,000 years came to an end.

By this point, the Tang was in its death throes. Zhu Wen took control of the court.

Move the capital to Luoyang.

What about Chang'an?

Burn it down!

Emperor Zhaozong (867 – 904)

After serving as the imperial center for 17 dynasties over 1,200 years, Chang'an would never again be a capital city.

In 907, Zhu Wen took the throne and the Liang dynasty was born, ending 290 years of Tang rule.

After the fall of the Tang dynasty, China entered another era of division.

In the north, the Chinese once again fought invading nomads. In the south, former Tang governors and local warlords established a dozen different kingdoms.

Unlike the earlier Age of Division, which lasted 369 years, the period of disunity that came after the Tang dynasty only lasted 53 years.

In 960, a general from a northern state unified most of China and founded the Song dynasty. This new dynasty made substantial economic, cultural, and scientific advancements.

But just when China was on the cusp
entering a truly modern age,
the Mongols came and
changed everything...

To be continued...

NOTES AND SUGGESTED READING

Pronouncing Chinese names can be very difficult. To keep things as simple as possible I've kept all Chinese names in pinyin, the standard phonetic method for transcribing Chinese words.

The only exceptions are names previously romanized according to different standards that are now very common. An excellent example is the name of the philosopher Confucius. If I were to write it in pinyin it would be spelled *Kong-fuzi*. Instead, I use Confucius, the name Jesuit missionaries gave him in the 16th century.

If you want to check your pinyin pronunciation there are a number of useful online resources available to you. An excellent web dictionary with audio capabilities can be found at www.mdbg. net. The Pleco app for iOS and Android phones allows you to check proper pronunciation.

In writing *Division to Unification in Imperial China* I relied on a number of Chinese-language sources. These include *History of China* by Tongling Wang, *The General History of China* by Simian Lü, *China: A Macro History* by Ray Huang Renyu, and *A History of Chinese Philosophy* by Youlan Feng. Many of these books are classic histories and have more information than I could ever fit into a series, much less a single volume. If you read Chinese these books are worth investigating.

While there aren't a huge number of English-language resources that address the period of Chinese history covered in this book in an accessible manner, *China between Empires: The Northern and Southern Dynasties* by Mark Edward Lewis and Timothy Brook is an excellent resource. I also suggest *Chinese Civilization: A Sourcebook, 2nd Edition*, by Patricia Buckley Ebrey, which collects original source material from Chinese history, including oracle bones, tax codes, and folk tales.

ACKNOWLEDGMENTS

To Sara, Elizabeth, Malcolm and Connor, Katelyn and Yifu, and many, many more children who have been born with a connection to China.

BOOKS IN THIS SERIES

Volume 1

Foundations of Chinese Civilization:
The Yellow Emperor to the Han Dynasty
(2697 BCE – 220 CE)

Volume 2

Division to Unification in Imperial
China: The Three Kingdoms to the Tang
Dynasty (220 – 907)

Volume 3

Barbarians and the Birth of Chinese
Identity: The Five Dynasties and
Ten Kingdoms to the Yuan Dynasty
(907 – 1368)
TO BE PUBLISHED APRIL 2017

Volume 4

The Making of Modern China: The
Ming Dynasty to the Qing Dynasty
(1368 – 1912)
TO BE PUBLISHED NOVEMBER 2017